Reflections
of
His
Love

"Inspiration for the Soul"

"From My Heart to Your Heart"

Reflections of His Love

Inspiration for the Soul

"From My Heart to Your Heart"

By
Carolyn Weeks May

E-BookTime, LLC
Montgomery, Alabama

Reflections of His Love
Inspiration for the Soul

Library of Congress Control Number: 2006927324

ISBN: 1-59824-231-8

First Edition
Published June 2006
E-BookTime, LLC
6598 Pumpkin Road
Montgomery, AL 36108
www.e-booktime.com

DEDICATION

This book of poetry has been compiled with much love for my family and many friends but ultimately, with love for my wonderful Father God and His precious Son, Jesus Christ, my personal Lord and Savior.

But I must mention and thank a few people who have truly impacted my life for good over these many years since I accepted Christ. If Jeanie Russo and her sister Judy Bolton had not come into my office to make their father's final cemetery arrangements, this book of poems would never have gone to the publisher. When they came in I could see immediately that they were very special people and by the time they left it seemed as if I had known them for years. The Lord burdened my heart to give them one of my poems when they were making the arrangements and when they read it they suggested that I needed to get them published. Then suddenly during the same year Jeanie's husband Salvatore went home to be with the Lord also, and at that time the Lord gave me the poem "This is not Goodbye" to give to Jeanie. I thank our Savior for my new friends and for the fact that they encouraged me to get these poems published.

I must also recognize my dear pastor who led me to my Lord, Ben Bravenac. Brother Edgar R. McCrary and his precious wife EvaLee, who were by my side all during my son Mark's recovery from being shot accidentally by his best friend, and then six months later when we almost lost our daughter Debbie, I will always treasure their friendship, and I must say that they not only taught the word but lived it out more than any two people that I have ever known. My friend Olivia Duke, who taught a bible study in my home in Houston for many years before we moved to East, Texas. My neighbors and friends Betty and Gene Weidemeyer and their boys John and Glenn, who lived across the street from us in our first home that we purchased, and we all came to know Christ within weeks of each other and went to the same church together for a number of years. My friend Ruby Joanne Kolajajck, who has been in prison ministry with me for years and has been such an encouragement and a blessing to my life. My precious friend Rene that I met through the prison ministry that I'm in, she has brought so much joy into my life (and the ladies in Esther's House, a Christian Halfway House in Dallas, Texas), and Louise my friend who has given her life to run the halfway house and mentor the ladies.

Grace and Dave Hill who became our friends when we were transferred to Dallas, and they were a special inspiration. My church, Gwinnett Community Church, and the Ladies in our Wednesday night bible study class, for their input regarding this book and for their prayers for me and for my family. Last but not least, due to being in the cemetery business, I have dealt with so many precious families at such a difficult time in their lives. It's always just when they have lost someone they love very much and each family is a true blessing to my life. I truly believe the Lord gave me many of my poems for these very families.

My Father, out of His goodness, blessed me over the years with many wonderful friends, too numerous to mention, for I have been transferred a lot and made such dear, dear friends wherever the Lord sent me. I thank God for each one and I know it was His faithfulness that enabled me to move so many times and yet make friends everywhere I went, (that I will have for eternity).

I dedicate this book to my Savior and my best friend, the Lord Jesus Christ, and to each of the friends that He has so graciously brought into my life as a special blessing. In some way each one has helped me to grow in my walk with the Lord, and I thank my God upon every remembrance of these dear ones.

Carolyn

Contents

Introduction 11

The Love of God 12
Reflections of His Love... 15
The Burning Bush 17
He's Been There and He Cares 20
Do People See Jesus in Me?...22
At the Foot of the Cross 24
The Flower of Life 27
Save Me a Spot Right Next to You...29
The Way of Your Choosing 31
A Friend..34
The Sweetness of His Presence 36
Lord Fill Me Up 38
The Blessings of God 40
Lead On, Dear Lord, Lead On...42
When Do We Call? 45
The Question 47
The Resting Place 50
I Love You 52
Through the Valley...54
Happy Birthday, Jesus...57
My Heart's Desire 59
The Glory Train...62
Don't Let Fear Get You Down..64
Jesus' Gentle Hands 66
Only God Can Change His Heart 69
To the End of Life's Journey 72
The Hand of God..74
Rush, Busy, Hurry 76
Rejoice My Downcast Soul...78
Momma of Mine...81
My Guardian Angel..83
Crystal Drops...86
Trust Him 89
No Exchanges...No Returns 91
Diamond in the Rough 93
Going Home 96

Contents

Humble Pie 98
No Higher Calling 100
Don't Live Your Life On Your Emotions 103
It's Raining 105
The Butterfly 108
Daddy 110
Lawd, I Been a 'Tryin 112
My Friend, This Is My Prayer for You 114
I Was Made for You, Lord 116
This Is Not Goodbye 119
No Room 122
Let Them Remember 124
Resisting Satan 126
Our Secret 130
Can You Praise Him? 132
Jesus I Love You 134
Let Us Be Thankful 137
Letting Go 140
Love the Unlovely 142
Meme 145
What Is Our Motive? 147
My Boss 149
Peaks and Valleys 151
Take My Life and Use It 155
The Little Thorny Briar 157
Feelings 160
Life Is Just So Busy, Lord 163
Praise Time 166
Take Me in Return 169
The Blood Is Here to Stay 171
I Wonder Who's Watching 174
Our Children 177
Tears 179
The Thief 182
All Is Not Right 185
Pray 188
Lord Show My Friend the Way 190
Making Memories 193

Contents

I'll Take and I'll Give..196
A Fit Vessel 199
The Real Meaning of Christmas..201
Loss Is Sometimes Gain..204
The Race..207
This Is Not Your Day 210
Total Surrender..213
The Captain of Our Ship 216
Storms..218
Safe in the Arms of Jesus 221
Bundles of Joy 223
Is Something Missing From Your Life? 225
Have We Come So Far That We've Forgotten?........................228
You Shall Light My Candle 231
Religion in a Box...233
Christmas Hustle Bustle 236
Sometimes I Don't Feel Saved..238
It's Over...240
Dear, Hurting Ones 242
The Master Painter 244
My Buried Treasure 246
The Lesson of Love..248
Yesterday, Today and Tomorrow...250
I'm a Know-So 253
Slowdown and Remember 255
It Was Such a Small Thing 258
Come Home...260
I Take the Blame 263
As We See Strangers Passing By 266
He's Always There...268
Is Your Heart Right? 271
Time Is Slipping Away 273
A Special Touch From You 275
Satan's a Subtle So and So...277
Hope 280
Easter Love..282

Topical Index...285

Reflections of His Love
Inspiration for the Soul

"From My Heart to Your Heart"

"Reflections of His Love" is a collection of poems and commentaries that I have been compiling over the years since 1985. The first poem that I ever wrote was "MEME" and it was written out of desperation, when my grandmother's birthday was coming up and I not only didn't have the money for a card but not even for a stamp. I had never missed her birthday since I was a little girl, and I wanted so badly to at least send her a card.

God is so good and while sitting at my desk at work and wondering what I was going to do, this little poem came to me, and I jotted it down and made a little homemade card. Then I borrowed a stamp from my boss, in order to mail it.

Well, from that time on poems started coming to me on a regular basis. For many years though I didn't know why the Lord was giving me all these poems, and I never showed them to anyone other than a few family members. Then after being in the cemetery and funeral home business for about 21 years, I started feeling the burden to write a poem for certain families that would come into my office when they had lost a loved one. Now, suddenly all these people started telling me I needed to get them published, and I just thought they were being nice. But I finally decided that if these poems could be a blessing to anyone, or perhaps bring glory and praise to my heavenly Father, then I would definitely pursue having them published, but only for His glory! He is so deserving of all of our praise and adoration and glory!

I pray that in some small way these poems might brighten your day, bring a smile to your face, lift your spirits, give you some spiritual insight that you didn't have before or just help you learn to praise your hurts away. If they bless you in any way then of all people I am most blessed, that our Father would give me such an awesome privilege.

May the Lord bless you as you read and receive Inspiration for Your Soul, From My Heart to Your Heart.

Carolyn May

THE LOVE OF GOD

Dear Saint of God, as a believer I am sure you must already know that the Love of God is totally unexplainable. It is completely indescribable and amazingly immeasurable. How can such a great love be available to every man, woman and child with no strings attached and it's absolutely free?

A love that would sacrifice God's only Son so that unworthy sinners could go to heaven and spend eternity with our awesome God. There are no words to describe it in our limited earthly vocabulary, and there is no way to truly comprehend it. A love that does not depend on us or anything we do, it is 100% unconditional and unmerited.

Once we become a believer in the Lord Jesus Christ, we still have the free will to choose to walk in His will and to have all His wonderful blessings and His abundant life that He had planned for all His children, or we can choose to walk in our own will and in our own way and be miserable, and miss out on all of His fantastic provisions. When you walk out of God's will and walk in your own, you don't lose your salvation, you lose your blessings. You can freely walk out of His will but you can never walk out of His love.

It is so wonderful to know we will never have to do anything to earn or merit God's love and as long as we live on this old earth we will never be able to accurately or completely describe, explain or measure THE LOVE OF GOD

If we would forget to praise You, Lord, even the very rocks would cry out.

THE LOVE OF GOD

The love of God is far above,
What our lowly minds can comprehend.....
We truly cannot grasp it, Lord,
A love that has no end.

It's higher than the sky,
It's deeper than the sea.....
It reaches down to every man,
It even reaches me.

A love that cannot be won or merited,
By anything we can do.....
But is freely given to all,
And is always trustworthy and true.

We can never wander away so far,
That Your love cannot reach us there.....
We may wander out of Your will,
But never out of Your care.

How is it, Lord, You endlessly give,
A love so boundless and free?
Father, knowing man.....
How can it be...how can it be?

So unworthy and so unlovely,
With no merit of our own.....
Yet we freely receive the greatest gift,
This world has ever known.

A love so undeserved,
And it's available to all.....
Even to the very vilest sinner,
When on Your name they call.

Jesus' death bought us Your love,
His blood, it covers our sin.....
So when You look at us, Lord,
You see "His" righteousness within.

THE LOVE OF GOD *Continued...*

Thank You, Father, for Your love,
And may I someday be…..
Able to graciously show Your love,
To others …as You have to me.

1985

Psalm 36:5,7 Your love, O Lord, reaches to the heavens, Your faithfulness to the skies. How priceless is Your unfailing love! Both high and low among men find refuge in the shadow of Your wings.

REFLECTIONS OF HIS LOVE

Reflections of His Love is one of the first poems I wrote back when we lived in East, Texas. I have always been so amazed that a King would come and die for the likes of me, and I believe that is why the Lord gave me this poem.

When you think of what our precious Savior went through for us on the cross and yet we take it for granted. And even though we take Him and His sacrifice for granted He never turns His back on us. He is always faithful to us even when we are not faithful to Him. How do you comprehend such love? The love of our Savior is reflected in everything He does for us. From His sacrifice on the cross, the example He set for us to follow, to the way He continues to provide for all of our needs.

We in turn should have the desire to be reflections of His love to the world and the only way to do that is to die to self and let Him live and minister to the world through us. Saint of God, what a privilege we have been given, to be called children of God.

Jesus, willingly shed His blood for us, would we be willing to do the same for Him, if it ever came down to it? I hope so. And yet, really all He asks us to do is LIVE FOR HIM. Hallelujah!

REFLECTIONS OF HIS LOVE

His leaving His throne in glory,
His leaving His Father in heaven above....
His dying for sinners like you and me,
...all reflections of His precious love.

Coming to earth to suffer such shame,
at the hands of such cruel men.....
all because of love ...He came,
and died to pay for our sin.

The innocent Lamb of God,
He came to pay the price.....
He came to shed His blood,
and to be our sacrifice.

No matter where we've been,
no matter where we go.....
no mountains ever too high,
no valley's ever too low.

...for the love of Christ our Savior,
to reach out and touch us there.....
for His outstretched arms to surround us,
with his tender love and care.

The ever flowing fountain,
that's flowing deep and wide.....
with reflections of His love,
in the flowing crimson tide.

The fountain that flows,
with our Savior's precious love.....
to the hearts of all His children,
from His throne in heaven above.

1985

THE BURNING BUSH

Dear One, have you ever felt like the little BURNING BUSH? Are there times in your life that you feel as if God could never use you? Do you feel that you just don't measure up to God's standards? Maybe there has been something in your past or present life that you feel like would keep God from using you and the devil keeps reminding you of whatever it is.

Well, remember, being used by God does not depend on us but on God, Himself. The Lord chooses whomsoever He will to use for His good purposes. It says in Romans 15:4 That whatever was written in earlier times was written for our learning, that we through patience and comfort of the scriptures MIGHT HAVE HOPE. And I am so glad that our Father put the old testament in His Word for it includes so many wonderful testimonies of how He chose to use so many of the Old Testament saints. And the really great thing about it is that He also includes their failures along with their successes, their sinfulness as well as their saintliness.

So whenever we feel unworthy or like the Lord surely can't use us, all we have to do is remember David, Samson, Abraham, Isaac, Jacob and many others that our Father used mightily in spite of their failures. Even Paul himself said in Romans 7:15& 19 I do not understand what I do. For what I want to do I do not do, but what I hate I do. For what I do is not the good I want to do; no, the evil I do not want to do- this I keep on doing.

It is so encouraging to know, our Father knows us, and loves us just the same. He loves us unconditionally, and if we but make ourselves available He will use us. Don't let your external circumstance get you down. Just like the Burning Bush, you never know when God is going to use you in a supernatural way, in a way that you never could have imagined. So wait on the Lord, wait patiently for Him and He will manifest Himself when you least expect it. The difference is that today He manifests Himself through His Holy Spirit. We have the indwelling Spirit and in the Old Testament times they didn't have that blessing.

Thank You Father, that You love and use us in spite of ourselves. Thank You for Your love, mercy, grace, patience, longsuffering, goodness, kindness, gentleness.....and the list just goes on and on. And thank You for the privilege of serving You.

Child of God, He loves you and He will use you, if you let Him.

God bless you as you wait on Him!

THE BURNING BUSH

A sad little shrub once existed.....
In the midst of the desert bare.....
Its' heart was nearly broken.....
And loaded down with care.

The fiery heat from the sun....
Danced upon the parched, dry ground....
And if you looked for miles.....
Not a blade of grass could be found.

Here and there a scrawny shrub......
Struggled to survive.....
And the little prickly bush.....
Wondered...why am I alive?

I'm not so much as a home....
For the bird to build her nest.....
And not with blossom fair or luscious fruit...
Have my branches ever been blessed.

I can't yield food for man to eat....
And my branches...were just not made.....
To give the weary traveler....
Some rest beneath my shade.

The lonely little bush....
Whispered sadly to the night.....
And found itself suddenly wishing,
It could be completely out of sight.

And then behold, one day Moses came.....
Leading his sheep across the land.....
The little bush burst forth on fire....
And Moses fell down upon the sand.

For God came to dwell in that little bush....
And He issued Israel's great commission.....
So, from that time forth...the little prickly bush...
Has held down quite a position.

All the passing ages….
Have been lit up and truly blessed…..
By the vision and the message…..
That came forth…from the "little bush"
…where God came to rest.

1985

Exodus 3:2B&4 Moses saw that though the bush was on fire it did not burn up. When the Lord saw that he had gone over to look, God called to him from within the bush, "Moses, Moses!"

HE'S BEEN THERE AND HE CARES

Dear child of God, it should bring us comfort to know, that nothing that we can go through on this earth, will take Jesus by surprise. For the scriptures in I Cor. 10:13 tell us that no temptation or trial has seized you but what is common to man. And God is faithful; He will not let you be tempted beyond what you can bear.

Whatever we are called to go through, Jesus has been there first. He knows all about our sorrows and our trials, and He will never be caught unaware. There is nothing we will be called to go through that He won't be right there with us. Psalm 55:22 says Cast your burdens on the Lord, and He will sustain you; He will never let the righteous fall.

The Lord wants us to let Him carry all our burdens, so when we get overwhelmed with our circumstances it is because we have failed to cast our burdens on Him, and LEAVE THEM THERE! Why do we want to carry our burdens when we don't have to?

Sometimes we feel like nobody understands what we are going through and nobody cares. In fact many times people ask how we're doing and then they act uninterested if we start to tell them how we're really doing. They just want to hear "FINE!" But Jesus is never too tired to listen and He cares. I Peter 5:7 says, Casting all your cares on Him for He cares for you, your adversary the devil, like a roaring lion, stalketh about seeking whom he may devour.

Dear Friend, walk with your hand in Jesus' hand and know that He always cares.

HE'S BEEN THERE AND HE CARES

We have a loving God who knows about,
Each trial and trouble sore....
Our friends and loved ones care,
But He cares even more.

He knows the grief and heartache,
And when we suffer loss.....
For He trod that same lonesome pathway,
And had to drag a cross.

He faced the same temptations,
That we face every day.....
There is no road that we can walk,
That He does not know the way.

Why do we fear the future,
When we should leave it in His hands?
He'll never expect us to bear...
More than we can stand.

Christ endured the affliction of the cross,
For He knew the joy in store......
He despised the shame,
But He loved His Father even more.

So, while we're passing through this world,
We know we'll suffer many things.....
But it's knowing who holds the future,
That makes our sad hearts sing.

Our Jesus knows the way,
Clear over to the other side.....
So until we make it home,
We can Trust Him to be our guide.

1987

Psalm 37:4-5 Delight yourself in the Lord, and He will give you the desires of your heart, commit your way unto Him and trust in Him also and He shall bring it to pass, He shall bring forth thy righteousness as the light and thy justice as the noonday sun.

DO PEOPLE SEE JESUS IN ME?

You know many years ago there was a great gospel song by the Imperials, called "You're the Only Jesus Some Will Ever See" and it really spoke to my heart. In this life we only get one chance to make a first impression and when we get that chance, what impression do we leave on that other person?

If what people see in our lives is the only impression that they get about Jesus, then what will they think of Him? Will they think, "Well, if that person is a Christian, then I certainly don't want to be one". Or will they think, "Gee, if that is what Christianity does for you, then how do I sign up?"

Another line in that same song says, "You're the only words of life some will ever read" Well, if our lives are a walking testament, what are they reading in our lives? Do they just want to slam the book shut or will they want to read it over and over?

Friend, remember your life has an impact on the lives of others, so, what impact are you having? Do you say one thing, but live another? If so you must start getting serious about your testimony for the Lord, or you will never be able to lead someone else into the kingdom of God. It all starts by loving others more than yourself, as the scripture says: Do all things in lowliness of mind, each esteeming others as more important than themselves.

Although the pages in your book may become ragged and torn, it's the message on each page that counts not the physical condition of the page. And when the book is completely unreadable from age and use, then the Lord will take us home to be with Him forever and our book will have a new glorified cover and pages that will last for all eternity. Hallelujah! Praise the Lamb! Just remember if He hadn't saved us, we would be a book without a cover and fit for nothing but to be thrown into the fire, where there will be weeping and gnashing of teeth.

God Bless You Friend as you seek to serve Him, and let Him write your book!

I Corinthians 10:13 My God is faithful and He will not let you be tempted beyond that you are able, but will also with the temptation make a way of escape that you may be able to bear it.

DO PEOPLE SEE JESUS IN ME?

Do people see Jesus in me?
Can they read Your word in my life?
Sometimes words are made flesh.....
And they walk before men in plain sight.

In my everyday walk....
Does my life speak for You?
The things that I say,
Do they always ring true?

If people are to know You, Lord,
Then I know my walk must be.....
Spotless and unblemished,
For all the world to see.

Does my light shine forth,
In this sin-darkened world....
Do I walk the straight and narrow,
Though Satan's darts at me are hurled?

Do I live just any way,
Or do I live what I believe?
My actions affecting others....
Then what must they conceive?

Will they see that Jesus lives,
And that He walks upon this earth....
In the form of one like me,
Since I received my brand new birth?

Father, if my life contains the only words,
That they will ever read of You.....
Then, please, let them ...every single word,
Be all and only true.

1985

Heb.12: 1-2 Therefore, since we are surrounded by so great a cloud of witnesses, let us lay aside every weight and the sin which so easily besets us and let us run with patience the race that is set before us, looking unto Jesus the author and finisher of our faith.

AT THE FOOT OF THE CROSS

Can you in your wildest dreams imagine, standing at the foot of a cross and seeing your precious son, badly beaten beyond belief, nailed by his hands and his feet, to that cross? Can you put yourself in Mary's place at the foot of the cross. Your son's blood dripping down. Even the other people who loved and cared about your son were standing there as well, but nothing could ease your pain. It's hard, probably impossible to even imagine it. For although we may have lost a loved one and they may have suffered some pain before they died, at least they weren't sent to their deaths because of the actions of others and they weren't unjustly paying for the crimes(sins) of others.

Our Father graciously sent His Son to die for us and Jesus willingly obeyed the Father's plan, even though He could have called 10,000 angels to get Him out of there. All because of love these things came about for our fallen race. So that we might be redeemed and have eternal life. Out of gratitude and appreciation, should we not willingly live our lives for Him?

Even though Peter denied knowing Jesus 3 times before the cock crowed Jesus, still forgave him and Peter still had his salvation.

This Easter let's meditate on Mary and what it must have been like. And even for His followers who were there. Paying for our salvation affected so many lives that we never think about. It caused a mother to see her son die and others to watch their savior die and Jesus had other family members it also affected. If we really only knew the extent of the whole thing, would we take it so lightly? I HOPE NOT!

AT THE FOOT OF THE CROSS

Don't you know His mother's heart was broken,
As she watched her Son die.....
And many others who loved Him,
Were also standing by.

The women were weeping and praying.
At the foot of the cross.....
Before this terrible day,
They had never suffered such loss.

Their one and only precious Savior,
Hung there slowly dying.....
And the soldiers were laughing,
But the women were crying.

The crowd stood there waiting,
For the soon coming end.....
Surely after such suffering,
Death would seem like a friend.

The crown of thorns pierced His brow,
And the nails in His feet and hands,
Satisfied all the heavenly Father's
Holy and righteous demands.

Why did one so kind and so gentle
Have to suffer such pain?
For after His death
The world would never be the same.

Or would it?

Through the sighing and weeping,
You could almost hear the angels sing.....
Rejoicing over the victory,
That was being won by their king.

For by His death Jesus had won
The victory over the grave.....
And now the door was opened,
For the lost to be saved.

Easter is not just dying the eggs,
And fun with family and friends,
It's the death and resurrection of our Savior,
To give us love and life without end.

Jesus brought a love to this earth,
It had never, ever known,
And He called out a special people,
To be all His own.

A people to tell the story.....
Of God's so great salvation plan,
Brought down to earth by Jesus,
For every woman, child and man.

This sin fallen world,
Praise God...was given life anew,
And my friend, if you don't possess it,
It's waiting for you. (In Jesus)

Happy Easter and remember what it's all about!

2006

THE FLOWER OF LIFE

Friend, if our lives were flowers in the garden of life, what kind of flower would you be? Would you stand out whether you were growing in a beautiful flower garden, or whether you were growing in a weed patch? Just as a beautiful, fragrant flower stands out wherever it has been planted, so our lives should stand out wherever we go.

Just as the beautiful blossom leaves a lasting, pleasant fragrance, so our lives should leave a beautiful, sweet-smelling aroma wherever we have been. But unfortunately some Christians, when they pass through our lives they are more like a weed. Weeds are considered a nuisance in our flowerbeds or in our gardens, something to be removed and discarded. Where flowers make a lasting, beautiful impression and even when the flower finally begins to fade and lose its' leaves, people are usually sad to see it go and actually wish that it could last a little longer.

Dear one, when its' your time to go will people be sad to see you go or will they be relieved? Whether through death or a move, our leaving should be a loss to those who have been around us. So, wherever the Lord has planted you, try to be the most beautiful, fragrant flower in that particular garden of life.

Bloom where God has planted you!

James 3:13 Who is wise and understanding among you? Let him show it by his Good life, by deeds done in the humility that comes from wisdom.

THE FLOWER OF LIFE

Our life is like a flower, that goes from bud to bloom....
It's woven like a tapestry...on God's own heavenly loom.

The bloom stays open for awhile, and then it slowly withers away.....
Even the leaves surrounding the bloom,
Start to droop in a sad-looking way.

Yet while a bloom is open, because of the way God has them made.....
They bring delight to everyone...before they begin to fade.

In fact, it makes one sad, when we do see the beauty fade......
Often wishing the death of the flower, could somehow be delayed.

Our lives should bring such beauty, into the lives of those nearby.....
That just like the bloom of the flower...it blesses each passerby.

Even if a little bloom, grows up in a briar patch.....
It has a special beauty, that a weed could never match.

For a flower never blends in with the weeds, but stands out all alone.....
Even if it's the only flower, the weed patch has ever grown.

Do we standout from the world, or blend right in with the crowd?
Do we bring a ray of Sunshine...or a dark foreboding cloud?

Have we brought a touch of joy, or perhaps salvation to the lost?
Have we shared and cared for others...no matter what the cost?

When our time on earth is gone...and it's time for us to go....
Will our lives leave a special fragrance, and perhaps a sweet afterglow?

When our hair has turned to silver, and our years have all passed by....
Will our Savior say, "well done, my child", when we meet Him in the sky?

1989

My friend, what kind of blossom will you be?

28

SAVE ME A SPOT RIGHT NEXT TO YOU

Save Me a Spot Right Next to You is a little poem, that I feel the Lord gave me as a means of encouragement to those families that have lost loved ones and have come to my office to make their final cemetery arrangements. I have always felt that my job is a ministry in itself.

If there is ever a time that families need love and encouragement, it is when someone they love very much has gone home to be with the Lord. Whether it was a sudden death, or a long illness before they passed away, it is never easy to go through the loss of a loved one. Saying goodbye, when we know we won't be seeing one another again for a long time is hard, for we are going to miss them so much, until we have that glorious reunion some sweet day.

Of course it is easier, when we know they have gone to be with the Lord, than when it is a person that we know had no relationship with Jesus.

This is just a little poem to remind us, that we and our friend or loved one will one day be together again, if we both know Jesus as our Savior. So, let's all make sure we have done everything on our part, that is humanly possible, to make certain all those we know and love have had an opportunity for that divine appointment. For without Christ our friend or loved one won't be filling that spot right next to us when we get home to heaven.

May the Lord continue to bless you as you seek to serve Him and to be His witness to all those you love and care about.

SAVE ME A SPOT RIGHT NEXT TO YOU

If you should get to heaven…..
A little before I do…..
I hope you'll save me a spot…
Right there next to you.

Since we've been together here on earth,
For such a long, long time…..
I hope that once you get your spot,
That You'll hold on to mine.

Being in eternity together,
I know will be so grand…..
And we can stroll all over heaven,
Holding Jesus by the hand.

I know that once we're there together,
We'll forget the time we've been apart…..
But until at last I arrive,
I'll hold you close to my heart.

So be sure and save me that spot…..
Right there next to you,
Sitting at the feet ….
Of the One so True…..

The One who died to save us….
Who died to set us free…..
The One whose precious face…..
We've been longing to see…..

So If you get there…..
Just before I do…..
Please, save me a spot…..
Right next to you.

But… I'll save you that spot,
Right there next to me…..
If I happen to get their first,
And that's a possibility.

See Ya Soon!   2005

THE WAY OF YOUR CHOOSING

When God created man he gave him a freewill to choose to accept Him or reject Him. So every person has a choice of going to heaven or to hell. And sadly because of pride, many will spend eternity in hell. They often stumble over the simplicity of the Gospel. It is so simple to understand that a child can comprehend it at a very young age, and yet adults will fail to accept it because they say it's too easy, there have to be some strings attached. They have to believe there is something they can do to get to heaven, that they can be good enough or do enough good works.

Jesus offers the free gift to all of mankind and yet some freely choose to reject the gift and try to find another way (of their choosing)to get to heaven.

Believers should take advantage of every opportunity to give the Gospel to people who need to know the Lord, for you never know when this could be the day that their eyes will be opened to the Truth. Without Jesus they'll spend eternity in hell, so let's try to give them every opportunity to make that life saving decision.

Father, give us a tremendous burden for the lost and dying souls. Put Your words in our mouths and You promised your word will not return void, but will accomplish what You want it to and prosper where You send it. Isaiah 55:11

Praise Your Name!

THE WAY OF YOUR CHOOSING

Do you know my Jesus?
The One with thorn pierced brow…..
Whose loving nail scarred hands,
Say, my child, I love you anyhow.

For I know you didn't know,
What you were doing then…..
You were crucifying the Son of God,
The Savior of all men.

But in this present day and age,
Men ignore God's Holy Word…..
Blindly going on with their lives,
As if they had never heard….

The Word that tells them…God sent His Son,
To be their sacrifice,
The precious Lamb of God…..
Gave His life to pay the price.

The price of freedom from our sin,
And it was paid for one and all…..
Yet sadly today some reject that gift,
They reject His loving call.

Don't you know it breaks His heart,
Seeing those for whom He gave His life…..
Rejecting His gift of love and salvation,
Instead choosing death, sin and strife.

He tried to let them know,
That He was their only way…..
But their ears were deaf to the truth,
Well, maybe another day.

But another day just may not come,
Today could be their last…..
So, I pray they won't come too late,
For then in hell they will be cast.

And then in hell they'll suffer forever,
With the devil and his crew.....
Instead of enjoying heaven's bliss,
They'll be drinking a bitter brew.

Sorrow and tears and suffering,
How sad...the way they chose.....
When heaven was theirs' for the asking,
Since the day that Christ arose.

1985

My friend, which way will you choose?

A FRIEND

Friends are a blessing from God, and they are someone who loves us unconditionally, just as God our Father loves us. And in order for us to be a friend, we must also be able to love others unconditionally just as we want God to love us.

It's so awesome that a friend is someone, where God has chosen to dwell; and it is God Himself loving us unconditionally through that person. The sad thing is, that we have many acquaintances, but few real friends, and I believe that is because so few have actually surrendered their lives to Christ. They have accepted Him as their Savior, but they have never learned to die to self and to let Jesus live, and unconditionally love through them.

Have we learned how to be a friend? We want everyone to love and accept us, but have we surrendered our lives to Christ, and learned to die to self, and to let Him live and love through us?

Until we become a good friend, are we really worthy of having good friends? Let's allow God to make us into good friends for His glory.

Are you a good friend, dear one, and if not why not? Surrender your all to Jesus today, and ask Him to empty you out of yourself, and to fill you up with Him, and ask Him to love others through you. And then you will enjoy a special relationship with other people that you have never known, and with God Himself as well. In fact, you can even turn your enemies into friends!

May God bless you as you seek to do His will and may He bless You with many friends and make you a friend to many.

Rom. 12: 21 Do not become overcome by evil but overcome evil with good.

Prov. 18:24B But there is a friend that sticks closer than a brother.

A FRIEND

A loving friend is worth a fortune, not in silver or in gold...
But their value is far greater, than mere words have ever told.

For a friend comes from the Lord, sent as a blessing to our soul,
And they meet a special need... since they make a half a whole.

For one is merely a single... but two becomes a pair.....
And life is a lot more fun...when our blessings we can share.

God uses friends to bring us joy, and to turn our frown into a smile...
Whatever the need may be... they'll go that extra mile.

A friend rejoices when we're happy...and they comfort and encourage us
When we're sad... they tend to our needs when we're ill...
And put up with us when we're bad.

A friend will keep our secrets, and will always cover our sin.....
In fact, they're called upon in many ways...again and again and again.

What kind of friend are we? Are we always on the take?
Or do we enjoy giving more...and a truly good friend make?

Do we love our friends when they're unlovely?
When they're sick....and down?
Do we try to win a smile...from their downcast frown?

Do we mend their broken hearts... Putting broken pieces back in place...
And finding all the pieces ...by God's amazing grace?

Are we always available to God...ready to do His will,
Being a blessing to our friends...ready to climb the highest hill?

Looking for nothing in return...but praising God...that instead of I it's we,
And by His grace... He not only gave me a friend,
But by His power...He made a friend out of me

1987

Prov. 17:17 A friend loves at all times.

Prov. 18:24 There is a friend that sticks closer than a brother.

THE SWEETNESS OF HIS PRESENCE

Isn't it amazing that even in our darkest hour we can still feel the presence of the Lord? And saint of God, if we can just trust Him until the storms be passed by, we will find a special joy awaits us on the other side of the storm.

If you are like me, there are times, when trials come into my life, that at first I start to worry and fret and wonder how in the world I am going to make it through. But God is so faithful, and He gently reminds me that He is right there with me and He is the One who will see me through. If I will simply lay my burden at Jesus feet, He will gladly carry it for me.

There unfortunately have been times when instead of giving my situation to Jesus, I would stay awake at night worrying, and all that did for me was make me feel worn out the next day. The sad thing was, I could have left the entire circumstance to the Lord and let Him take care of it. Besides, worrying doesn't change a thing and it only serves to get us down and discouraged.

The only way to peacefully make it through the storms of life, is to take our burden to the Lord and leave it there. To hide in the shelter of His wings until all the storms be passed by and a new day dawns.

Help me Father, to trust You enough, to leave all my burdens and cares in Your hands, and not to get in your way.

Psalm 4:8 I will lie down and sleep in peace, for You alone, O Lord make me dwell in safety.

Psalm 121:3-4 He will not let your foot slip He who watches over you will not slumber; indeed, He who watches over Israel will neither slumber nor sleep.

THE SWEETNESS OF HIS PRESENCE

The journey I travel, as I make my way homeward,
May seem at times to be a dark and lonely way…..
Troubles may surround me and grief may tear at my heart,
And I question, "How much sorrow can one feel in just one day?

Yet even in the darkest hour…the sweetness of His presence,
Somehow I feel within my anxious heart…..
And suddenly I find…a quiet peace, a kind of joy,
Another day begins…a brand new start.

At times tears may stain my pillow…as at night I softly cry,
And I feel my heart within me is just about to break.
Then the dear Lord reminds me…He'll be with me
Through the night,
And right beside me when morning comes and I awake.

January 27, 1987

Romans 8:38-39 For I am persuaded that neither death, nor life nor angels…nor principalities nor powers, nor things present nor things to come…neither height nor depth nor any other creation shall be able to separate us from the love of God which is in Christ Jesus our Lord. Praise His wonderful name!

Psalms 30:5 His anger endureth but a moment, in His favor is life; weeping may last for the night but joy cometh in the morning. Hallelujah!

LORD FILL ME UP

Isn't it amazing that the more we learn to die to self, the happier we can become. When Jesus fills us up it enables us to love more deeply, care more sincerely and to be more real. Sometimes when we do things in the flesh, we get no enjoyment from it for self gets in the way. Jesus brings us joy, so when He fills us up, our lives are filled with blessings.

The world cannot understand the kind of joy and blessing that comes from dying to self and being filled up with Jesus can bring. It would make no sense to them, because self is everything to the unbeliever. The world wants self-gratification, not realizing, that will never give them any real satisfaction or any real peace, joy or happiness.

Saint of God, aren't you just thrilled, that you've found the secret to living, and it's dying!

Galatians 2:20 I am crucified with Christ, and I no longer live, but Christ lives in me. The life I live in the body, I live by faith in the Son of God, who loved me and gave Himself for me.

LORD FILL ME UP

Lord, sometimes it hurts me so.....
To look inside and see,
That there's no room for You,
For I'm all filled up with me.

And although I hear You calling,
"My child, come lay your burden down".....
I keep right on acting like,
I haven't heard a sound.

Then suddenly Your love,
Comes piercing through the gloom.....
Although I've often told You,
That in my heart You'll find no room.

But Your love is the light,
That brightens up my day.....
And when I'm lost in darkness,
It helps me find my way.

Yes, Your love is the key,
That unlocks my heart.....
And when I'm out of options,
I can find a new place to start.

So may I be emptied out of myself,
And be filled up with You.
May Your precious name be glorified,
In all I say and do.

Lord, fill me up with Your Spirit,
So that all this world will ever see.....
Is You and Your sweet love,
Whenever they look at me.

April 7, 1987

Galatians 2:20 I am crucified with Christ, nevertheless I live, yet not I but Christ lives in me, and this life I now live, I live by the faith of the Son of God, who loved me and gave Himself for me.

THE BLESSINGS OF GOD

The blessings God has waiting for His children, we can't even begin to imagine. The word tells us eye has not seen, nor ear heard, neither has entered into the heart of man the things that God has prepared for those who love Him.

I'll bet it's so grand that He deliberately doesn't want to tell us the full extent of it, or people would be trying to get there faster. Jesus says in John 14, "In my Father's house are many mansions, if it were not so, I wouldn't have told you. I go to prepare a place for you, and if I go to prepare a place for you, I will come again and receive you unto myself, so that where I am there you may be also", and Thomas said, "Lord, we don't know where You're going and how can we know the way?", Jesus said, "I am the way, the truth and the life and no one comes unto the Father but through me."

What a blessing to know that we have a Father who loves us so much that He has unbelievable accommodations waiting for us when we get home to heaven.

I don't believe our natural minds can comprehend what the Lord has waiting for us when we get there, but it has to be fantastic, and we can thank Him ahead of time for the wonderful home we have waiting for us, in that land beyond forever.

Carolyn

Are you excited yet? I am!

THE BLESSINGS OF GOD

The things God has for His children,
We can't possibly comprehend.....
For eye has not seen, nor ear heard,
Neither has entered into the hearts of men.

The sights in heaven we shall see,
I know that they'll be so grand.....
But what could possibly measure up,
To holding our Savior's hand?

There will be no more sickness and no more pain,
No more trouble or sorrow.....
No more regrets over yesterday......
And no more fears for tomorrow.

When we step upon the glistening sands,
Of heaven's golden shore.....
We'll be seeing our dear loved ones,
Who've already gone before.....

And more than mansions on hilltops,
Or streets paved with gold.....
More than all the rewards,
That heaven can hold.

The joy that they'll bring.....
Well, it just won't compare,
To being with Jesus.....
For all eternity there.

We'll be casting all our rewards,
At His precious feet.....
For we'll have no other desire,
When our Savior we meet.

All will be peace,
And love for all time.....
To think...knowing I'm Jesus',
And Jesus is mine.

1987

41

LEAD ON, DEAR LORD, LEAD ON

Lead On, Dear Lord, Lead On, is a poem that I wrote when after being in the cemetery and funeral business for 21 years, a few years before I was going to retire, my company that was the fourth largest in the industry in the U.S. sold out to the largest cemetery and funeral home company in the world. I had been planning on retiring at 57 years of age and the sale of the company changed all my plans. The new company cheated us out of our retirement, that our old company had set up for us and I could no longer even think about retiring.

I ended up taking a job in Atlanta, Georgia working with some people I had known for years, but there have been rumors that the company is selling out and at 61 years of age that could be a very scary thing, but with the Lord on our side we have no need to fear the future. He promises to supply all of our needs according to His riches in glory by Christ Jesus. All we have to do when trials come our way is just hold more tightly to His hand and let Him lead the way.

We should have complete confidence in our security. If Jesus took care of our salvation and our eternal future, then we can know that He is capable of taking care of our daily needs as well. There is no problem He can't solve, no question He can't answer. Nothing we may encounter is too hard for the Lord to take care of it for us. We can face anything that comes our way with Jesus by our side.

He promises to meet our every need.

Thank You Jesus, for the peace, that comes from knowing You're in control of our every situation.

We love You, Lord, so lead on!

LEAD ON, DEAR LORD, LEAD ON

Knowing my Savior…is walking beside me,
Makes the pathway of life much less forlorn…..
Just knowing He's there…calms all my fears,
Right in the midst of the storm.

He always leads my way,
Along the pathway so rough…..
And then He lovingly carries me,
When I cry, "Lord, it's enough".

Through nights long and lonely,
With no friends in sight…..
He says, "My child, follow this way,
And I'll be your light".

The Savior's always there,
In heartache and loss…..
Paying our dues,
No matter the cost.

When I'm feeling so blue,
And things seem dark and drear…..
He says, "I'll never leave you,
I'll always be here".

The thorns of life…..reach out,
To tear our hearts in many pieces…..
But since Christ goes on before me,
My peace just never ceases.

Then one day I felt as if,
I could go on alone without harm…..
When suddenly I noticed,
His flesh had been cruelly torn.

You're bleeding Lord, I cried,
Did You do that for me?
He said, "do not worry or fret my child,
I did it most gladly".

LEAD ON, DEAR LORD, LEAD ON *Continued...*

I fell on my face at His feet and cried,
Lead on…dear Lord, lead on forever …..
No mountain's too steep or valley too deep,
If we travel on together.

2006

Exodus 15:13 In Your unfailing love, You will lead the people You have redeemed. In Your strength You will guide them to Your Holy dwelling.

WHEN DO WE CALL?

Isn't it amazing that some people call on the Lord when everything is going great and they have no problems. For they are the type that if they're in the middle of a trial or they're going through a valley experience, they are almost mad at God the Father and don't have anything to say to Him. It's as if they are pouting, thinking, I don't deserve this.

Then there are those people who never seem to call on the Lord at all unless they have a problem or they are going through some tough times, then they can't contact Him fast enough. When things are going well for this type of person, then the Lord doesn't seem to come to mind.

Are you like either one of these two believers? If so, then I hope the first thing you will do is get your priorities in order. God is a jealous god and He wants our attention when things are going great or when we're in the midst of a trial. He wants us to talk to Him without ceasing, whenever and wherever we can. He loves us and wants a real relationship with us. He's our dearest love and if our spouse or boyfriend or girlfriend never talked to us unless it was to complain or to ask for something, how would that make us feel? Well, don't you think God feels the same way?

From now on let's talk to our Father, Best Friend, Savior, Lord and King, day and night, when we sit in our house, when we go walking or driving, when we get up and when we go to bed, let's be in a constant conversation with Him. Let's not just go to Him when we want or need something or when we want to complain, let's have an attitude of gratitude and praise all day long.

Father, how we praise You, for being Who You are, for putting up with us and all our many failures, and yet providing for all our needs, and especially for loving us unconditionally.

WHEN DO WE CALL?

His love for us remains the same,
In clear and stormy weather…..
He's the Rock…our Sure Foundation,
Never shifting ever.

No matter how we treat the Lord,
He loves us just the same…..
He's with us day and night,
Through the sunshine and the rain.

He's always there to turn to,
Whenever things get dark and bleak…..
And we cry out in sorrow,
Because our faith is getting weak.

He'd love to hear us call Him,
To thank Him now and then…..
Instead of always calling,
To tell Him just how rough it's been.

For we seem to call a lot,
When we need a helping hand…..
But we let our conversation slide,
When things are going grand.

Let's take time to talk to Jesus,
When things are really swell…..
Not just when we've lost our job,
Or we're not feeling well,

From the lips of grateful children
Whom He holds very dear……
Rejoicing, praise and worship,
Are the things He loves to hear.

So, let's have an attitude of gratitude,
And let's fill our hearts with song….
We have so much to thank God for,
We could praise Him all day long!

1985

THE QUESTION

If we knew all the answers we wouldn't have to walk by faith, and there would be no need to trust the Lord.

I have to admit as a child of God, I have so many questions that I want to ask my Father, when I get home. But until that time I just have to trust Him and have a complete childlike faith in Him.

Under the direction of the Holy Spirit, we should be able to find the answers to most of our questions in the Word. If there are any answers that we cannot find in Scripture then we will just have to wait until we get home to get the answers. We are to walk by faith and not by sight, and a perfect example of walking by faith is Moses wandering around in the wilderness for 40 years with a bunch of mumbling, complaining Israelites.

But saint of God, isn't it a joy to know, that we really have no need to doubt or worry or even question our loving heavenly Father, when we know He always wants what is best for each one of His children.

Thank You Father, that I can rest in You, knowing that You have all the answers and You are working everything out together for good in my life. Help me, to live day by day, one moment at a time. Trusting all to Your loving care.

I Corinthians 13:6-7 Love does not delight in evil but rejoices with the <u>Truth</u>. It always <u>Protects</u>, always <u>Trusts</u>, always <u>Hopes</u>, and always <u>perseveres.</u>

THE QUESTION

There are questions whose answers,
We may not get to know.....
Until our Father up in heaven,
Tells us why it was so.

For while we're on this earth,
We walk by faith and not by sight.....
Trusting in the Lord to lead us,
By His power and His might.

It's not our good works,
But His death on the cross....
That won our salvation,
When He paid the cost.

The cost of our freedom,
From death, sin and shame....
He dreaded the payment,
But He paid it just the same.

The payment was His death,
Upon that cruel tree.....
Yet willingly He hung there,
And died for you and me.

It's beyond our imagination,
How He left His glorious throne.....
To hang upon that cross,
And to die there all alone.

Although there were crowds of people,
Standing everywhere.....
The suffering and the shame,
Only He could bear.

How could His heavenly Father,
Send One so precious to die.....
For unworthy sinners,
Like you and like I?

To watch His beloved Son,
Being falsely accused.....
And then time after time,
Being beaten and abused.

We'll never know the answers,
Not this side of heaven anyway.....
But until we get there...we can praise and thank Him,
For forever and a day.

Thank you Father, that we have the privilege of praise.
Help us to use that privilege to praise You forever.

Thanks be unto God...for His unspeakable gift!

1985

THE RESTING PLACE

The Resting Place is a poem that came to me not long after my son Mark and my daughter Debbie almost died, both within months of each other. During the time in the hospital waiting room I could only make it by picturing myself hiding under the Lord's wings. I actually pictured myself as a baby chick, snuggling up under its mother's wing. It was exactly as Psalms 57:1-2 said. I could just imagine a little chick right in the midst of a terrible storm, hiding under the shelter of its' mother's wings.

Can't you just picture the rain pouring down and the terrible winds blowing the momma hen's feathers in every direction, and yet the momma hen pulls the little chick ever closer up under her wings. The little chick doesn't even fret for it knows it's momma is going to protect it no matter what. It feels completely secure.

Saint of God, we should be exactly the same way with our heavenly Father. We should feel completely secure under His wings, when all about us the storms of life are raging. Rest in Him and know that He will protect you until the storms be passed by.

Psalms 2:12 Blessed are all who take refuge in Him.

Psalms 18:2 God is my rock, in whom I take refuge.

Psalms 46:1 God is our refuge and strength.

Psalms 91:2 He is my refuge and my fortress, my God in whom I will trust.

THE RESTING PLACE

There's a place where peace and joy abide,
A place for the weary of heart.....
And for those who've lost their way,
They can find a new place to start.

It's far from the cares of this sin worn world,
You can find that place to hide.....
It's under the shadow of the Almighty's wings,
...you can there forever abide.

No clouds are in the sky.....
But grace and love abound,
It's at the end of God's sweet rainbow...
That this sacred place is found.

He promised us a refuge.....
Right in the midst of the storm,
Where there's no need to fear,
And certainly no cause for alarm.

You can feel so very secure,
Resting under His wings.....
That the sad and weary heart,
Once again begins to sing.

So, until the storms be passed by,
And the sun shines anew.....
You can find your shelter in the Lord,
For He cares for you.

1985

Ps.57:1&2 Have mercy on me, oh, God, have mercy on me, for my soul,
trusts in You, In the shadow of Your wings will I take my refuge until
all these calamities be passed by.

I LOVE YOU

It's so hard to say goodbye to someone we love. Especially when you've known one another or perhaps been married to one another for so many, many years. But when we weep at the time of their departure, we are weeping tears of joy for the time we had together, and tears of sadness for the time we'll be apart. And yet, we'll have precious memories to keep in our hearts, until that time when we'll be together again.

We cannot question God's will, and our friends and loved- ones are all on loan to us while they're here. They belong to God, and we can thank Him, for the time that we had them in our lives, and that we will be together again one day, in that land beyond forever.

We need to always remember that if our friend or loved one could come back, they wouldn't want to, instead they would want us to join them in paradise.

II Samuel 12:23 David said, Can I bring him (his baby with Bathsheba) back again? I will go to him, but he will not return to me.

Psalm 30:5 His anger lasts only a moment, in His favor is life. Weeping endures for the night but joy comes in the morning.

I LOVE YOU

When someone we love suddenly passes away....
the first thing we wonder..
"Why couldn't they stay".

But God has a special place, our eternal home....
with joy unspeakable at the foot of His throne.

Why, we ourselves would want to go....
if we knew what was in store.....
right across the Jordan, on heaven's golden shore.

If our loved ones who are there, "by some means",
we could ask, "don't you want to come back?"
They'd say, "No way, I'm having a blast!"

Why would I want to leave a place of such pleasure?
For it's like ending a search and finding lost treasure.

No, I'd never go back, but I'll be waiting for you....
and I'll be shouting "Hallelujah!"
when you come into view.

Then once you get here, you won't want to leave....
when all of these blessings at last you receive.

But I can't tell you more, for you might want to rush.....
and God has His special time for each one of us.

So for now, it's goodbye and I'll see you soon....
just beyond the stars, the sun and the moon.

And I'll say "I love you", can't wait to see your face...
and that look of amazement .....when you get a glimpse
of this place.

Won't it be grand?

2005

53

THROUGH THE VALLEY

Dear Saint of God, when you're going through one of the many valleys that we are called to go through in this life, there's never a cause for alarm for we know our God is with us. No valley is too deep or too wide for our Father to see us through to the other side.

We may get frightened now and then for our old flesh is so weak, but our Father is there with us, wherever we are and whatever we are doing. In fact we couldn't get away from Him if we wanted to. Our loving God has promised us that He will never leave us nor forsake us.

We may not have much materially in this life but the only thing that really matters is Jesus. If we have accepted Him as our personal Lord and Savior then we have everything we need to make it through. In fact not only will He provide for all our needs while we're here on earth, but He will also take us home to glory when our time on this old earth comes to an end. We may wander out of His presence but never out of His love. And even when we do wander away, He is always waiting with open arms, when we get tired of wandering and turn around to look for our Father.

Thank You Father for Your faithfulness to us even when we are not faithful.

II Timothy 2:11-13 Here is a faithful saying: if we died with Him, we will also live with Him; if we endure, we will also reign with Him; if we disown Him he will also disown us; if we are faithless, He will remain faithful, for He cannot disown Himself.

THROUGH THE VALLEY

To the depths I have been,
To the depths I can go.....
Since I have Jesus with me,
That's all I need to know.

So, when I find it hard to trust,
And my faith is feeling weak.....
Please, help me, Lord, to patiently,
Be still and let You speak.

For in Your still, small voice,
Your comfort will come.....
At the breaking of the day,
Or at the setting of the sun.

And I don't really need to know,
Just what lies ahead.....
For I know that You'll be with me,
So there's no need for fear or dread.

The valley may be narrow, deep, dark and long,
Do I have the faith to make it through?
Blindly I'll take Your hand and go at Your command,
For all I'll ever need Lord... is You!

In this life I have nothing...except You, Father God,
And I know... that all Your Words... are ever true.....
So whenever I'm afraid...I'll hold tighter to Your hand,
For I know Your promises...will always see me through.

Whether You lead me to the top of the highest mountain,
Or down to the depths of the deepest sea.....
I'll trust You Lord, regardless of the circumstances,
For I know my Savior only wants what's best for me.

1985

Psalms 23 The Lord is my shepherd, I shall not want, He maketh me to lie down in green pastures, He leadeth me beside the still waters, He restoreth my soul, He leadeth me in paths of righteousness for His names sake. Yea, though I walk through the valley of the shadow of death, I will fear no evil, for thou art with me, thy rod and thy staff they comforteth me, thou preparest a table before me in the presence of mine enemies, thou anointest my head with oil, my cup runneth over. Surely goodness and mercy shall follow me all the days of my life and I shall dwell in the house of the Lord forever.

HAPPY BIRTHDAY, JESUS

Christmas came this year, and just like every other year, it made me stop and think about, how the real meaning of Christmas is becoming more and more forgotten, and I think it is hitting me harder every year. This year it was so discouraging, to hear how many stores won't allow their employees to say, Merry Christmas to their customers. They have forgotten that there would be no Christmas or Holiday if it wasn't for Jesus' birth.

I never dreamed that in America we would see a war on Jesus. The schools won't allow any Christmas Carols and most of the stores play secular Christmas music over their intercoms.

The world has forgotten that JESUS IS THE REASON FOR THE SEASON.

All Christians should take a stand and remind the world (at least the one around them) that Christmas has always been the Christian's time to celebrate the birth of the King of Kings and The Lord of Lords and without His birth there would be no reason to celebrate CHRISTMAS!

Everything about Christmas has become too commercialized. It's not even about Jesus, it's about shopping and parties and having fun (and there's nothing wrong with that if you include Jesus in it all) to the exclusion of celebrating the birth of the Savior of the World.

Next year I pray that all Christians will take Christmas more seriously, and that they will show the world the real meaning of Christmas.

HAPPY BIRTHDAY, JESUS

Jesus, it's Your birthday,
And no one seems to care…..
It seems their just so busy,
They have no time to spare.

It seems like years ago,
Your birthday meant more to people then…..
But things somehow have changed,
I really don't know why or when.

I guess folks have gotten so busy,
They just don't have time for You…..
And after all this time of year,
There's just too much to do…..

…too much to do to celebrate,
the birthday of a king…..
the birthday of our Savior,
Who gave us everything.

Through Your birth You saved us,
By Your hand You'll guide us…......
By Your death you'll raise us.
To heaven You'll take us.

Jesus, it's Your birthday,
And yet You're the gift giver…..
You willingly gave Your life,
So that we could live forever.

I pray the world will remember,
Your birthday this year….
And that should be our reason,
For spreading Christmas cheer.

Forgive us for forgetting You,
And the reason that You came…..
For through Your birth (and death),
This world will never be the same.

December 2005

America, let's put Christ back in Christmas!

58

MY HEART'S DESIRE

It seems to be so easy for us to desire the vain things of this world. Especially when everyone else has it or everyone else is doing it. But it doesn't take long for a believer to find out, that the material things of this world can never satisfy our hungry heart. Only Jesus can satisfy our soul. When we accept Christ as our personal Lord and Savior, we become a spiritual being and our spirit is satisfied with spiritual things.

The material things of this world are not wrong to have, as long as they don't have a hold on you, and as long as you have your priorities in order. But you will find that the things of this world can bring us a moments joy but they cannot and will not bring us any lasting happiness, joy or peace of mind. In fact, some people overextend themselves financially in order to get the things of the world, and then they not only don't bring happiness but they bring unhappiness, stress and unrest because they're worrying about how they are going to pay for them. A perfect example of someone getting their priorities mixed up was Solomon. The Lord blessed him with more wealth, wisdom, fame and everything else than any other person in history, and yet even though he knew it all came from the Lord, before it was over with he allowed his wives and concubines to set up idols in the temple and he started worshipping with them. The scriptures tell us, Let him that thinketh he standeth, take heed lest he fall.

Believers need to set their hearts and minds on things above and not on things on the earth. The Word tells us in Matt.6:33 Seek first the kingdom of God and His righteousness, and then all these other things will be added unto you. So that tells me when the desires of my heart line up with the Word, and I ask my Father for spiritual blessings and for my needs to be met, then He's going to bless me with other things as well.

We already know that many times when we ask for our needs to be met, He knows and gives us our wants as well.

What a good God we have. He knows our needs even before we voice them and He knows our wants and often graciously blesses us with them, just because He loves us.

Father, let my desires be Your desires for me and let Your desires be my desires for me.

MY HEART'S DESIRE

Don't let my heart in sin desire,
The vain things of this world…..
The things like gold or silver,
Or even precious pearl.

And may I never seek,
The worthless praise of men….
For it will only lead to pride,
And that of course is sin.

May I never long for fleeting,
Fortune, fame or money….
But put within my heart a craving,
For pure milk and honey.

The pure milk and honey,
Of Your precious, holy word…..
Let it be the only thing,
That satisfies my soul.

Then let me always long for love,
and joy and peace within my heart…..
Gentleness, goodness, and faith,
Will give us a perfect place to start.

Lord, Give me a desire… to do Your will,
Whatever it might be…..
for I know Your will…will always, be what's best for me.

Until the day You call me,
To my home beyond the skies…..
May I always see by brother,
Not through mine…but through Your eyes.

My heart's deepest desire… is the hope,
That every person I may see,
If they only see You in one life,
Lord, Let it be in me.

1985

MY HEART'S DESIRE *Continued...*

Philippians 1:9-11 And this is my prayer; that your love may abound more and more in knowledge and depth of insight, so that you may be able to discern what is best and may be pure and blameless until the day of Christ, filled with the fruit of righteousness that comes through Jesus Christ, to the glory and praise of God.

THE GLORY TRAIN

I, to this day don't know how I came up with The Glory Train, but I know that it always reminds me, that Jesus did it all for me, and for you and for every other person in this world. He paid for our tickets and all we have to do is get on board The Glory Train and we can ride for free.

People are without excuse, their tickets to heaven have already been paid for and all they have to do is get on board. Yet so many refuse the ride, there are those who say, no, I'll take some other train, a later train or a train taking some other route. Some people question the free ticket. They want to pay their own way. They think nothing worth having can possibly be free. They think to themselves, I'll just work a little harder so that I can pay for my own ticket.

If all these people only knew. The devil has them blinded and if they don't have the scales removed from their eyes very soon, the train will have left the station and they'll be left behind. Or else they'll get on a train going in the wrong direction or taking the wrong route.

So be sure to invite everyone you know to come along and get on board THE GLORY TRAIN, while they still have time.

Don't forget to thank Jesus for your free ticket. It was free to you, but it was extremely costly for Him.

What would we do without our wonderful Savior?

Romans 6:23 The wages of sin is death but the gift of God is eternal life through Jesus Christ our Lord.

THE GLORY TRAIN

I heard the man say,"the Glory Train
Is a comin' round the bin"....
An'once it passes by this way.....
It'll never be comin' agin;

So when it arrives at the station...
Git on board before it's too late....
Cause if yore a wantin' to go to Glory...
You shur can't afford to wait.

You kin hear its' whistle a blowin'....
Somewhere on down the line.....
So git yore ticket ready....
Cause yore a runnin' outa time.

The trainmaster's a takin' tickets...
As each soul goes a passin by....
He's hollerin' "this train's a bound for Glory...
She's a headin' fur the sky.

Jesus has paid our way.....
So we kin ride fur free.....
He's already purchased the tickets...
And there's one fur you and one fur me.

So come an git on aboard the Glory Train...
It's a comin' round the bin.....
Don't ya be throwin' yore ticket away...
Cause it won't be passin this way agin.

GET ON BOARD!!!

February 11, 1987

Rom.5:15 But not as the offense, so also is the free gift. For if by the offense many are dead so by the free gift of God's grace, many are made alive.

Rom.6:23 The wages of sin is death but the gift of God is eternal life through Jesus Christ our Lord.

DON'T LET FEAR GET YOU DOWN

Dear Friend, I have found that over the years, there were times in my life, that for a season I have let fear control me and my actions. I wish I could say that I have always been strong enough to commit all my fears to Jesus and leave them there, but that has not always been the case. One thing I have found out though, is that God is so faithful, and there have been times when He conquered my fears even before I asked Him to. The times that I have held onto my fears for some unknown reason, on the other side of the circumstance, God has been so kind about letting me know He still loves me and everything is going to be alright.

The sad but funny thing is my Father also has a way of reminding me, that if I would have left everything in His hands and not worried, things could have and would have gone so much easier for me. And you would think that after going through these kinds of trials several times that I would have learned my lesson, and I wish I could say that was the way it was. But God is good and He knows we are weak, and that we are going to try and carry our own load, instead of giving it to Him to carry and never taking it back. Sometimes, it's almost like we struggle with Him, trying to take it back so we can worry some more.

I must say I'm getting better about leaving things in His hands. Besides it's so foolish not to do that all the time, when from experience I know how much easier life is when I'm not carrying unnecessary burdens.

With God and His angels fighting our battles for us, why do we want to try to fight them ourselves? It just makes sense to leave the battle in the hands of the forces who can win. In fact, who have already won.

Hold on to His hand, hold on for dear life, and never let go!

DON'T LET FEAR GET YOU DOWN

When going through life's trials,
And I'm in deep distress…..
Do I faint from fear…..
And Satan's sure duress?

Or do I cast my cares on Jesus,
And continue my journey on ahead….
Knowing I can't lose my way,
For by His hand I'm led?

When fear grips our hearts,
And it just won't go away…..
No matter how many times,
We rebuke Satan in a day…..

Don't let that ugly fear,
Even start to get you down…..
For remember your Heavenly Father,
Has His angels all around.

The angels are in a constant battle,
With Satan and his crew…..
And there's no way on earth,
They can get the best of you.

So, the next time that ugly fear….
Intrudes into your life,
Simply keep on trusting Jesus…..
And He'll make everything alright.

Then when your heart is pounding…..
And your palms are wet like dew,
Just hold on a little longer,
And you'll make it safely through.

Saint, Don't give up!

1985

Prov. 3:5-6 Trust in the Lord with all your heart and lean not on your own understanding, in all your ways acknowledge Him and He will direct your paths.

JESUS' GENTLE HANDS

Can you just picture what it must have been like on this earth when Jesus came upon the scene. It was a world without love or caring, everyone just looking out for themselves. People were probably longing for someone to care. I always felt that they saw something in Jesus that they had never seen in anyone else, genuine gentleness, love and concern, so people were drawn to Jesus when He walked upon this earth, and when He went home to be with the Father, He left the responsibility of being His hands to the believers He left behind. Since the time of His ministry on earth, all those who put their faith and trust in Jesus as their Savior are given the opportunity to serve the King of Kings and the Lord of Lords.

To think that God's own Son, would allow us the privilege of being His hands, reaching out and ministering to a lost and dying world. We have an awesome responsibility and need to take it very seriously.

Most people never even stop to think about why we're here. They don't realize that God created us to be His servants, but due to our free will we have the choice of being a servant of the king or a servant of the devil. My friend, whose servant are you? Make your choice today, don't delay for you may not have tomorrow!

Matthew 4:25 Large crowds from Galilee, the Decapolis, Jerusalem, Judea and the region across the Jordan followed Him.

JESUS' GENTLE HANDS

When Jesus walked upon this earth,
He had a gentle, loving heart.....
And gentleness flowed out in His speech,
Mending broken lives and broken hearts.

He had gentle hands that brought healing,
To the blind, the sick, and the lame.....
They followed Him almost everywhere,
For His gentle touch they came.

One day they nailed those gentle hands,
To a rugged, cruel tree.....
Would His gentle touch be lost forever,
For sinners like you and me?

No, His touch had changed the world,
And it would never be the same.....
He taught lessons of love and kindness,
Never taught before He came.

Love was the law of His kingdom,
And it began to spread throughout the land.....
And the world's unloving, unkind ways,
Began to feel the touch of His gentle hand.

That gentle touch is felt today,
Giving souls a brand new start.....
And when one dies to self,
It gives Jesus a place in their heart.

Those gentle hands still comfort,
Heal and guide the souls of men.....
But now instead of from without,
He does it from within.

We are now to be His hands,
His loving touch to others.....
So reach out in Jesus name,
And gently touch another.

1985

67

JESUS' GENTLE HANDS *Continued...*

Matthew 15:30 Great crowds came to Him, bringing the lame, the blind, the cripples, the mute and many others, and laid them at His feet and He healed them.

ONLY GOD CAN CHANGE HIS HEART

Have you ever prayed for someone and really believed with all your heart, that what you were praying for that person was definitely what was best for them? So, Lord, if this is what is best for them, then why don't You hurry up and do what I'm asking you to do?

After a few days, weeks, months or years we start thinking, this is just ridiculous, Lord, when You know what I'm asking You to do in his or her life is in their best interest, then don't You think it just makes sense to go ahead and change them? Or at least *Convict* them of their *need* to change, for after all it's going to be the best thing for everybody, best for our whole family, or the whole office, or the whole church, or the whole growth group or bible study.

Sometimes it never occurs to us, that perhaps we are the ones who need to do the changing, and we have been so focused on the splinter in the other person's eye we have been totally unaware of the huge log in our own eye.

Proverbs 10:12 Hatred stirs up anger but *love covers* a multitude of sins.

I Cor. 13:4-7 Love is patient, love is kind, it doesn't envy, it doesn't boast, it's not proud, it's not rude, it's not self-seeking, it's not easily angered, and keeps no record of wrongs. Love does not delight in evil, but rejoices in the truth. It always protects, always trusts, always hopes, always Perseveres. Let's ask our Father to change our hearts first and then we can see clearly how to help others in their walk.

God bless you as you seek to serve Him.

ONLY GOD CAN CHANGE HIS HEART

I want so much to see,
my husband walking with the Lord…..
but getting him to do it,
I seem to find quite hard.

If he'd just be in the place,
where the Lord wants him to be…..
I know he'd be much nicer,
to others and to me.

Lord, what can I do,
to make him change his ways?
I've cried and prayed and pleaded now,
for lo, these many days.

What! Quit trying to change him,
when I know what I want is right?
but that's like giving up,
and going down without a fight.

I guess I've nothing to lose,
after all the tears I've cried…..
after all these many years,
and all those tricks I've tried.

For alas I find,
after trying all these years…..
(and when he didn't change his ways,
I cried so many tears).

That I can never change his heart,
no matter how I try…..
no matter how I beg or plead,
no matter how I cry.

For only God can change his heart,
so help me to leave my husband's in Your hands…..
and concentrate "myself",
on meeting Your righteous demands.

ONLY GOD CAN CHANGE HIS HEART
Continued...

And while You're changing hearts,
don't make me wait in line.....
the very first one that You change,
Dear Lord...please let it be mine.

December 17, 1986

TO THE END OF LIFE'S JOURNEY

Like so many other poems that I wrote back in 1985-1987, they were written during a very difficult period in my life. And yet as I have mentioned before it was as if God Himself were carrying me through the circumstances. He was giving me everything I needed to make it through the hard times.

It's really not the hardships in life that make us feel so uncomfortable here. I think it's just the world itself. It's as if we are on a journey through a foreign country and we don't speak the language. We are on a trip and we enjoy it a little bit, but we never really feel at home, staying in a foreign country, in a foreign hotel, in a foreign bed. we have some fun seeing the sights, but after a few days we're ready to go home. We're ready to see our loved ones and friends, and to be in familiar surroundings, to eat some good old home cooked food, and that can never happen as long as we're away from home.

We're on a journey through this world to the next, and with Jesus as our guide, we can be confident that He will lead us safely home. But as long as our journey lasts, He will be with us, leading us, guiding us, protecting us, and providing everything we need to make the journey home a safe and successful one. He will even show us how to use our time on the journey the most effectively and the most profitably. Remember that on this journey, we can build up rewards for our future, if we know how.

We have the greatest guide in all of creation, so there is no way He will allow our trip to be a failure or disaster. We are the only ones who can mess up our trip, but that won't happen if we just let our guide lead the way and we never fail to follow and obey our guide.

Have a blessed journey friend!

TO THE END OF LIFE'S JOURNEY

You'll be my strength, Lord,
And You'll be my stay.....
To the end of life's journey,
You'll lead the way.

On paths dark and dreary,
You'll be my light.....
To the end of life's journey,
Through the darkest of night.

When the pathway gets rocky,
And the footing's unsure.....
To the end of life's journey,
You'll keep me secure.

As the road gets rough and rugged,
And I'm filled with alarm.....
Then I remember... to the end of life's journey,
You'll keep me from harm.

Through valleys and over mountains,
In the shadow of death.....
To the end of life's journey,
When I take my last breath.....

...I know you'll be with me,
Your grace saw me through.....
To the end of life's journey,
Face to face with You.

1985

THE HAND OF GOD

As a believer in the Lord Jesus Christ, if we take the time to consider God's creation, we realize how truly awesome it is. You can see His handiwork all about you. Everywhere you look!

Some of His creation displays His power and might, and then much of it displays His tenderness and love. I think some of His creation even reveals His sense of humor, don't you?

If we'll be quiet, we can let His creation speak to us and it can tell us so much about our Father and Who He really is.

The believer and the unbeliever alike get to enjoy the many blessings of our God and it seems as though everyone would realize just by viewing His creation that there has to be a God.

Romans 1:20 For since the creation of the world God's qualities---His eternal power and divine nature have been clearly seen, being understood from what has been made, so that men are without excuse.

Thank You Father for all Your many blessings!

THE HAND OF GOD

As you walk through a forest,
of tall stately trees…..
you can almost hear God whisper,
in the cool, gentle breeze.

And when you gaze up into heaven,
At a brightly shining star…..
you can see His awesome power,
no matter where you are

When you're strolling in a garden,
Filled with blossoms oh, so fair…..
You can smell the scent,
Of something sacred in the air.

You can see the pretty blossoms,
And watch them go from bud to bloom…..
They can brighten up your life,
And chase away the gloom.

They have a fragrance so unique,
For it's made by God alone…..
And each bloom in the garden,
has a fragrance all its' own.

The mighty roar of the river,
as it winds through the hills…..
or the song of the robin,
perched on a window sill.

His power and His might,
His gentle, loving touch…..
are revealed all about us,
in the things we love so much.

The hand of God is seen and felt,
His voice is often heard…..
by all of His creation,
without a single word.

1986

RUSH, BUSY, HURRY

Rush, Busy, Hurry was written at a time in my life, when I was trying to balance my work and home life with my Church life and ministries. And I would feel guilty if I had even a fleeting thought, that I was worn out, and that I dreaded having to prepare a dish for Wednesday's covered dish supper or I didn't see how I was going to get this special project organized in time.

Life at times just seemed so hectic. And yet those were some of the most joyful times of my life. It's just that sometimes we allow ourselves to get involved in so many things, that we suddenly realize that we don't really have time for the most important thing, our time with the Lord, one on one, quiet time alone with our Savior.

When I think about how I would feel, if those that I love didn't really have any quality time for me, if they just managed to squeeze in a few minutes for me now and then. It really makes me wonder how the Lord feels, when we just squeeze Him in a few hurried minutes once in awhile.

And yet the most important and profitable time that we have, is that time spent with our Lord. To think that the King of Kings and the Lord of Lords willingly takes time out for us, and that nothing that we have to tell Him is too unworthy for Him to take time out to listen.

So dear friend, let's never be in too much of a rush, or be too busy or in too much of a hurry, to have our priorities straight, when it comes to our time.

Slow down!

II Timothy 2:4-5 No one serving as a soldier gets involved in civilian affairs-he wants to please his commanding officer. Similarly, if anyone competes as an athlete, he does no receive the victor's crown unless he competes according to the rules.

RUSH, BUSY, HURRY

Rush, rush, rush, got to get to church on time…..
Got to try and hurry, it's almost quarter past nine.

Busy, Busy, Busy, running here and there…..
Being so involved for the Lord, in everything and everywhere.

We've got to go and do our thing, we've got to work for God…..
After all we already know, it's a fast-paced path we trod.

Hurry, Hurry, Hurry, not a minute to spare…..
Finish supper…rush right off, to Wednesday night church and prayer.

Covered dish supper, I've got to bake a pie…..
If I didn't take a dish, how could I look them in the eye?

We've got a revival coming up, and I just realized…..
I've got to get a nursery together, and get it organized.

Got to find time to study, there's not enough hours in the day…..
I teach a bible class, guess I'll have to study on the way.

Isn't it sad how many believers,
Believe the more you do the better you are.
If they don't do everything they possibly can,
Then their crown won't have a star.

They think they've got to go and do, and then they've got to do and go…
After all they're working for God, and they've got to make a good show.

If you're behind….you can catch up, by simply slowing down….
Rushing makes us lose our smile, hurrying replaces it with a frown.

So take time to read God's word, and to pray throughout the day…..
Then rearrange your priorities, and you've found a much better way.

1985

REJOICE MY DOWNCAST SOUL

Rejoice My Downcast Soul is a poem, that I wrote at a time in my life, when I was finding myself feeling down and discouraged. After going through so many trials and difficulties such as Mark, my son being shot and almost dying, my daughter Debbie almost dying 6 months later, losing our home, business and automobiles, and yet having the joy of the Lord. Then suddenly it was such a strange thing to be going through this period of unexplainable sadness.

The Psalms have always been the medicine for the soul, and I'm so glad that in many of the Psalms you can tell the author (whether it was David or some other author), was feeling very low, but most of the Psalms if they don't start out with praise, in some part of the Psalm they usually turn to praise.

As I have mentioned before, it is almost impossible to praise the Lord and stay down and discouraged. Praise just has a way of lifting your spirits.

I wrote this poem as a prescription for treating depression and discouragement. Praise is a means of finding your way home.

Remember to rejoice, for regardless of your situation, this too shall pass.

Phil. 4:4 Rejoice *always*, and again I say *rejoice*!

REJOICE MY DOWNCAST SOUL

Rejoice my downcast soul.......
And look to the Savior above,
Rejoice in knowing Jesus.....
And for abiding in His love.

Rejoice when darkness dims the skies.....
Through the sunshine and the rain,
On days that are filled with happiness.....
On days filled with sorrow and pain.

And though at times your burden.....
May seem far greater than you can bear,
Rejoice my downcast soul.....
For you know you're in His care.

Rejoice my downcast soul.....
You've been given eternal life,
No more sorrow...no more pain.....
No more sin and strife.

Rejoice when friends forsake you.....
And loved ones turn away,
For when you opened up your heart.....
Jesus came in to stay.

Though oftentimes you feel like a stranger.....
In a faraway, unfriendly land,
Rejoice my downcast soul.....
And just hold more tightly to His hand.

Rejoice my downcast soul.....
The dawn is beginning to break,
Heartache and tears will all be gone.....
When at last you awake.

Rejoice when you remember.....
That this could be the day,
The day that Jesus is coming back.....
To take us home to stay.

Keep your eyes on the eastern sky…..
Keep listening for the trumpet's sound,
Rejoice my downcast soul…..
For you'll soon be homeward bound.

1987

Psalms 42:5 Why are you downcast, O my soul? Why so disturbed within me? Put your hope in God, for I will yet praise Him, my Savior and my God.

MOMMA OF MINE

Back in 1986 I wrote a poem for my momma and sent it to her for Mother's Day. I was hoping to let her know how very grateful to the Lord I was, that He had blessed my life with such a wonderful mother. What greater blessing can we have, than loving parents and grandparents?

I always felt that I was blessed above all people by the family that I had. My parents didn't accept Christ as Savior until I had known the Lord for a few months, and I had kept on begging them to come to church. To get me off their backs they made up their minds that they would go one time and then tell me it wasn't for them, but the rest was history. They both accepted Christ and never looked back. We had so many wonderful times together in our church until my husband bought a business in another city and we had to move away.

But growing up by the grace of God, even though my parents didn't know Jesus personally, they were good worldly people. They couldn't have been more loving. It's just that after they both accepted Christ, I knew that love was coming from Jesus.

Thank you so much Father God, for that MOMMA OF MINE, She's the greatest and I love her bunches!

MOMMA OF MINE

There are no proper poems, no songs with proper lines…..
That fit the way I feel, about that – Momma of mine.

Pretty as a picture, and oh, so good and kind…..
No where this side of heaven, could I ever find…
Another- Momma like mine.

She's an earthly angel, sent from God above…..
To shower those around her, with her special kind of love.

Love from God Himself, channeled through a believer…..
And it leaves a special imprint, on the blessed receiver.

I know her heart's been broken…..probably many, many times,
But she doesn't show it, that Momma of mine

She's made life so much sweeter, and all my burdens are lighter….
Why, just by her presence, the darkness is brighter.

And when she gets to heaven, she'll have a special crown…..
The Lord has saved for only those….who spread His love around.

Then when it's my turn, to enter heaven's gates…..
I won't be a bit surprised….when I see what awaits.

Waiting to welcome me, at the head of the line…..
With arms held open wide…will be that- Momma of mine.

And when around God's throne,
We have question and answer time…..
I'll ask the Lord why I was so blessed,
To have that precious …Momma of mine.

1986

MY GUARDIAN ANGEL

Many years ago when we were living in East Texas, I had gone to work as office manager for a company called Texicolors, Inc. I had been a housewife for many years but due to some extreme financial reversals it became necessary for me to take a fulltime job.

I was sitting at my desk typing one day, when I looked up and glanced out my window. As I did so, I saw a lot of beautiful puffy white clouds moving very rapidly across the sky, and it seemed as if you could just imagine God's angels enjoying an opportunity to play on the beautiful puffs of white. I could easily visualize their taking a break from their satanic warfare and having some fun frolicking among the clouds.

Then I thought wow, my angel has really had a fulltime job with me as their assignment, and so far, they've done a great job. If anybody ever deserved a break it would definitely be my guardian angel. It would take volumes to let you know about all the times from childhood on, that my angel had to work overtime. I really want to look them up when I get to heaven, and tell them that I know that I was probably a tough assignment, and that I truly appreciate all the hard work they had to put in guarding my pathway and keeping me out of trouble.

Aren't you glad that our God is so wonderful and that He has His awesome angels, (His own special creation) looking after us wherever we go. Our very own private bodyguards you might say.

Thank you Father for our guardian angels and the faithful service they put in guarding your children.

Psalms 91:11-12 And He shall give His angels charge over thee, to keep thee in all thy ways, and they shall bear thee up in their hands, lest thou dash thy foot against a stone.

MY GUARDIAN ANGEL

Looking at the clouds,
I can almost faintly see.....
Some of God's sweet angels,
Peeking back at me.

I can just imagine,
They're playing in the sky....
Floating on the puffs of white,
As they go sailing by.

I guess they need their wings,
To fly among the stars.....
To play and sing and praise the Lord,
And fight satanic wars.

Just think those precious beings,
Sent by God on high.....
To keep and guard our pathway
To the sweet, sweet by and by.

Sometimes you can almost feel,
The whisper-soft brush of their wings.....
When you've had a close call,
And your heart's left afluttering.

I'll bet the angels stand amazed,
After watching us here below.....
That our loving, righteous God,
Could love such creatures so.

You know, when I get up to heaven,
I want to find my angel unaware.....
And thank him for the job he did,
While I was in his care.

For I know I've been a tough assignment,
And kept my angel on the go.....
So when I get home to heaven
I want to let him know.....

....how much I truly appreciate,
the overtime he had to put in.....
and all the hard fought battles,
that he never failed to win.

1985

CRYSTAL DROPS

The poem CRYSTAL DROPS came to me one day when I was sitting in my den and looking out at the rain. At the time we were still living in our home in East Texas. As I was looking out across the pasture and watching the beautiful rain fall I thought to myself, our God is just so wonderful in every way.

We were losing our home due to the bad economy in Texas back in the eighties, but we had not had to move out yet. Due to such hard times, we had no money to go out or to go anywhere for that matter. We barely had enough money for food. We were losing our business and everything but the clothes on our backs, but it turned out to be one of the best times of my life.

By not having the financial means to go out, other than to work or to church, it makes your senses tune in to new things. I am ashamed to say that I had never really meditated on God's creation and in turn had never truly appreciated it the way I should have. When you do take the time, to take in the beauty of all that our God has created, it makes you wonder what the beauty of heaven is going to be like. After all we are living in a fallen world, and yet it still has such wonder.

When you think, that God not only created all this for us, but He also knew exactly what it would take to sustain His creation. Our God is an awesome God!

Dear One, why don't we take more time to enjoy our Father's creation, and to let Him know how much we truly appreciate all He has done for us, in giving us such a grand temporary home. It really shouldn't take having hard times, in order for us to take the time to enjoy these blessings and to let our Father God know how much it means to us.

Isn't our God just wonderful? I think so!

Thank Him, thank Him, thank Him and then thank Him again!!!!

Read all of Genesis 1

CRYSTAL DROPS

It rained today…..
Those Crystal Drops,
God sends to the plains,
And the mountaintops.

To water the earth,
When its' thirsty and dry…..
To renew its' strength,
And to stop its' cry.

Sometimes…..it rains a lot,
Sometimes…..just a little,
Sometimes it makes a river,
Sometimes just a puddle.

But God has a reason,
For just certain amounts…..
And remember…to Him…..
Every single drop counts.

He sends the drops of water,
So flowers and trees can grow.
He sends it so the river…
Won't dry up and lose its' flow.

He knows the bird…..
Make its' home in the trees,
And the fish love to swim,
In the deep blue seas.

Everything on this old earth,
Needs water to survive…..
The Lord knows just how much…..
And when it should arrive.

God made the water….
He made the earth too,
So, He knows just how much it takes,
To keep the earth looking new.

Little tiny drops…..
Oh, so crystal clear,
Without those Crystal Drops…..
There'd be nothing here.

1985

Psalms 107:35 He turned the desert into pools of water and the parched ground into flowing springs.

TRUST HIM

Dear child of God, it is so easy to trust God when things are going our way, but it seems to be a different story when trials and temptations suddenly seem to be coming from every direction. But what kind of God do we have? We are supposed to trust Him completely, with everything we have and everything that we are. As parents we want our children to trust us at all times. Through the good times and the bad, the happy times and the sad, the easy and the difficult times, at all times we want our children to confidently believe we want what is best for them.

We must believe our loving God knows and cares about each sorrow we bear and each burden we carry, and He tells us, (as the old song says) "Take your burden to the Lord and leave it there. If you trust and never doubt, He will surely bring you out. So, take your burdens to the Lord and leave them there." God never promised us a life in this world without any trouble or pain, look at what Jesus went through when He lived on this earth, and nothing we could ever go through could even come close to comparing to His sufferings and hardships. And to think He came to earth knowing ahead of time what He would be going through, and all because of His love for us. Trust is love and love is trust.

James 1:2-4 Consider it pure joy, my brothers, whenever you face trials of many kinds, because you know that the testing of your faith develops perseverance. Perseverance must finish its work so that you may be mature and complete, not lacking anything.

TRUST HIM

We must trust Him when it seems…as if we might have lost our way.
And the thunderstorms of life, have dimmed the brightness of our day.

When we've lost sight of Calvary…and just how much it cost,
And it seems we've reached our limit…of heartaches, grief and loss,

Trust Him when we've lost those things, that seemed so very dear…
And we cry out for comfort, and no one seems to hear.

He knows every sorrow and the heartbreak that we feel…..
For He's been there before us…and He knows it's oh, so real.

No matter how long before we turn to Him, in all our grief and pain…
He's always ready to comfort us…when we call out His name..

Trust Him for He's there, with arms held open wide…..
Where amidst the storms of life…we can run and hide.

We can take our refuge in the shadow of His wings…..
Till the storms be passed by, and our heart begins to sing.

Trust Him for He cares for you….and He wants to carry your load,
He wants so much to walk with you, along life's lonesome road.

He never leaves us or forsakes us…He never turns away,
If we feel lost and lonely…we're the ones who've gone astray.

Take His hand and never let go…as long as you're in this life,
For He's the only one who can lead us, through the shadow of
Death to life.

1989

NO EXCHANGES...NO RETURNS

No Exchanges...No Returns was originally intended to be a peppy little song. Instead I never got around to writing the music, and so it became a poem. And it was written during a time when Satan had truly been ferociously attacking my mind and my emotions. I personally believe that is his favorite battleground and it takes special weapons to fight this battle.

What did Jesus do when Satan attacked Him? He quoted scriptures at him. He did not revile him, but He used the most powerful weapon available against him. We sometimes forget how powerful God's Word really is. It says in Hebrews 4:12 That the Word of God is alive and powerful, and it is sharper than any two-edged sword.

Next time you have a spiritual battle to fight, remember to put on the whole armor of God in Ephesians 6:13-18. My friend, it is so important to memorize scripture for those times when you may not have your Bible handy when you need it for some sudden attack. You must be ready at all times.

God Bless you Dear One as you stand your ground.

II Cor. 10:3-5 For though we live in the world we do not wage war as the world does. The weapons of our warfare are not carnal, but mighty through God to the pulling down of strongholds, to the casting down of imaginations, and every high thing that exalts itself against the knowledge of God in our minds and bringing every thought into captivity to the obedience of Christ.

NO EXCHANGES ... NO RETURNS

There's a war going on.....
In the battlefields of my mind...
Not of flesh and blood....
But one of the spiritual kind.

The devil whispers in my ear.....
Trying his best to get me down....
But the Lord's angels are armed and ready....
On my spiritual battleground.

I may be scarred and bleeding.....
But Jesus has won the victory...
He fought and won the battle....
That day at Calvary.

He paid the price of my salvation....
He did it all for me.....
So, devil, just get on back.....
For Jesus has set me free.

You may launch an attack.....
From the front or from the rear....
But the Lord is the Victor.....
So I have no need for fear.

The end has been decided.....
The countdown has begun.....
Satan, you've been defeated!
Your time at last has come.

So....Get back Satan.....
NO EXCHANGES...NO RETURNS!
Jesus has won the battle....
Why won't you ever learn....to
Get back Satan?
NO EXCHANGES...NO RETURNS!

1986

I Peter 5:7 Be sober be vigilant for your adversary the Devil, like a roaring lion stalketh about seeking whom he may devour.

DIAMOND IN THE ROUGH

Have you ever thought about the fact that a beautiful diamond, like one that you might see in a very fine piece of jewelry, before it becomes that beautiful diamond, it starts out as an ugly old piece of carbon? In order for the ugly lump of carbon to become a beautiful diamond, it must be taken from the darkness of the mine and then it has to be cut and polished by an expert diamond cutter. The diamond is definitely not beautiful in its' natural state. It takes a lot of work to make it fit for use as a diamond in a piece of jewelry.

Our lives are the same way. In our natural state we can be quite unlovely, but after we accept Christ as our Savior (we're removed from the darkness of the mine) and the Lord starts to chip away at all the ugliness (sin and strife) in our lives, He, by the power of the Holy Spirit, transforms us into something beautiful and fit for His service.

Sometimes the cutting and polishing can be very painful, but once the process is complete, the newfound beauty causes one to forget about the difficult process that had to be gone through.

Our Father God is the diamond cutter and we are the diamonds and He knows exactly what it takes to make us into a beautiful diamond fit for His use. He wants us to be a diamond that will shine for one and all, one that will glorify Him with its' beauty.

So saint of God, when the Father is working on you, just know that He loves you and that the trial, pain or sorrow you may be going through, is working together for good in your life, it's making you into the person that He wants you to be.

Romans 8:28 All things work together for good to them that love the Lord, to them that are the called according to His purpose.

DIAMOND IN THE ROUGH

In times of stormy gales,
And deepest gloom…..
When your poor heart aches for rest,
And finds no room.

When your faith is tried to the limit,
So it would seem…..
And you pray that soon you'd awaken.
For this just has to be a dream.

You must remember in your heart,
And don't forget…..
That your Father God,
Is just not finished with you yet.

For the diamond in the rough,
Will never shine…..
But first it must be taken,
From the darkness of the mine.

Then in the hands of the cutter,
The blows must fall…..
If the diamond is to shine,
For one and all.

The amazing thing about a diamond,
Is that with each blow…..
Though once it was dull,
It takes on a brighter glow.

So with each blow,
That comes into your life…..
Falls away some unnecessary,
Ugly sin and strife.

In the loving hands of the Father,
You'll find peace that you've never known…..
When at last the Master finishes,
the cutting and polishing of the stone.

1985

DIAMOND IN THE ROUGH *Continued...*

James 1:2-4 Consider it all joy, my brothers, whenever you face trials of many kinds, because you know that the testing of your faith develops perseverance. Perseverance must finish its work so that you may be mature and complete.

GOING HOME

The thought of dying can be very frightening and I have always felt like birth and death are so similar. In birth you have a human being, coming out into an unknown environment. They may be just a baby but it is still a type of jumping off into the unknown. Well, when we go home to be with the Lord, it seems like it is another type of birth. We are entering our new environment. We become a baby again, as far as facing the unknown is concerned. For just like that baby (being born into this world), doesn't know what to expect, we don't really know what to expect when we leave this earth and arrive in heaven.

It's almost as if we are being born again. The big difference in this birth and the first one, is that with the first one, we don't know what kind of family or lifestyle we are being born into. It may be a very trying and difficult life, and yet the Lord will be with us regardless, if we accept His Son as our Savior. Whereas, we know that heaven is going to be grand for all those who have placed their faith and trust in Jesus. We have been given several descriptions in our Bible and it I'm sure it will be even more awesome than what we read, for scripture tells us,* that eye has not seen, nor ear heard, neither has entered into the heart of man the things that God has prepared for those who love Him. We will probably be speechless for a period of time upon arrival.

But GOING HOME was written to put hearts at rest about the GOING HOME experience.

Help us not to be afraid, Lord, we trust You with everything else, help us to trust You with our Home Going. It just has to be the ultimate thrill!

I Corinthians 2:9-10 *See above Verse 10 says, "But He has revealed it unto us by His spirit".

GOING HOME

Oh, dear child of God near Going Home....
Don't be afraid you're not alone.
Death is only a door in the dark,
Through which...when open shines the brightest spark...
All the way home.

You're loosed from bondage in this body of clay,
To join that glorious reunion on Homecoming Day...
Carried up, up and away... by the angels of the King.
"Welcome into Glory", you can hear them sing.
All the way home.

You'll be welcomed by angels and saints who've gone before,
Introduced to the King on heaven's golden shore.
And then dear soul, to hear Him say at last,
"Welcome home, my child, your dark days are past".
You're finally home!

Oh, most precious suffering one,
The battle's finally over...and it's been won!
Remember your valley experience, is not a leaving...but arriving.
So, now just rest in Jesus...no more need for striving...now that you're
home.

Soft footsteps of angels...come to carry you home.
Up....above sun, moon and stars...to the foot of God's
Throne. Jesus has brought you each step of the way....
Through the valley of death to the brightness of day.
He brought you all the way home.

1989

Psalms 116:15 Precious in the sight of the Lord is the death of His saints.

HUMBLE PIE

Dear One, are we truly humble or do we just think we are trying to be humble? When we walk in the spirit we don't have to try to be humble, it comes naturally. It's not an effort we make, it's a way of life.

Do we consider ourselves pretty important, or do we consider others as more important than ourselves? We need to be so careful about who we are, who we really are. In fact, do we even know who we really are?

Do people see Jesus in us? Do people want to be around us or do they avoid us? Are our lives a magnet or a repellent? Do we draw people to Jesus or turn them away from Jesus?

It is so easy to judge others and not to see our own sin. But if we are walking in the Spirit, then the Spirit will convict us of any sin that is in our lives and we will be fit vessels for the Lord to use to help others find their way.

I believe there are many things that we think are so important to God and that when we get home to heaven, we'll find out that they didn't really matter at all. He's concerned about souls. Let's be more concerned about a person's soul than about their works. Once they come to know Christ, the Lord will take care of any changes they need to make.

There are times that we need to be very careful, about trying to straighten out other Christians we see involved in things we feel they shouldn't be involved in. The scriptures let us know in Galatians 6:1-3 Brethren, if someone is caught in a sin, you who are spiritual should restore him gently. But watch yourself, or you also may be tempted. Carry each other's burdens, and in this way you will fulfill the law of Christ. If anyone thinks he is something when he is nothing, he deceives himself.

Dear Saint of God, let's be very careful regarding what we do with the life God has given us. Let us live it for His glory.

Philippians 2:3-4 Do nothing out of selfish ambition or vain conceit, but in humility consider others as better than yourselves. Each of you should look not only to your own interests, but also to the interests of others.

HUMBLE PIE

Do I by thoughtless things I do, turn men away from God?
When in my heart….. I thought I cared, what lonesome path they trod.

I thought it so important, not to cuss or smoke or drink…..
That it didn't really matter what that poor lost soul might think….

When I set down my list of rules, whether verbal or unspoken…..
And gave those critical looks and glances…when one of them was broken.

Then an unkind word said in haste, a slight slip of the tongue…..
Or judging "his" behavior…when really I'm the one.

I must judge myself and the deeds I do, and not to make men stumble….
and love all men…just the same, for only then will I be humble.

The things I thought to be alright, I now find out are sin…..
And it breaks my heart to know….I've hurt the very souls I sought to win.

So lets let Jesus do the saving, and the Holy Spirit will reveal…..
Anything that's in their lives, that goes against His will

We must simply tell the story, of Christ's death on Calvary's tree…
And just how much it cost….that salvation for you and me.

So, let us truly love them…and remember them in prayer,
And God will save and keep them…until that meeting in the air.

For only God can do the changing, if any needs to be done…..
And all we can do is watch and pray, and point the way to the Son.

1985

Romans 14:13 Let us not therefore, judge one another anymore, but judge this rather: that no man put a stumbling block or an occasion to fall in his brother's way.

Being a servant in the family of God has better benefits than any worldly position could ever offer. Benefits that the world itself knows nothing about. Sadly, if everyone knew there would be long lines of people trying to take advantage of the opportunities available. My friend, in this world today, there are so many miserable people, in fact some of the very people that you would expect (from the world's point of view) to be the happiest. Some of the people that have the most of this world's material possessions, such as money, big houses and fancy cars, and some even have high-powered jobs in the most prestigious industries, yet they are so unhappy that you hear about them committing suicide or divorcing or doing some foolish thing that gets them sent to prison.

I truly believe that much, if not all of their unhappiness and misery is brought on by their not having a saving knowledge of the Lord Jesus Christ. Of course there are even Christians that are terribly unhappy, because they have never learned how to have a close personal relationship with the Lord. They are going to heaven when they die, but they are not living the wonderful, abundant life that the Lord intended for us to live. They don't know how. It's tragic.

Once you totally surrender your all to Jesus and let Him take full, complete control, you will find a new life in Christ, that even many Christian's don't know about. It's like when you give your life away to Jesus, He gives you a whole, new, abundant life. Not always abundant in the things of this world, but in the things that matter, and only the blessings of God can ever truly satisfy. The things of this world can NEVER satisfy. They may bring some fleeting happiness or satisfaction, but not everlasting joy.

When you become a servant of the Lord, it is our highest calling and the most rewarding, you can't go wrong enlisting in the service of the Lord and the benefits are awesome!

Enlist today my friend.

NO HIGHER CALLING

There can be no higher calling,
Than to bow and kneel before the throne......
Of the One Who died to save us,
And Who'll never leave us alone

When you have no where to turn,
Just fall down at Jesus feet.....
And you'll find His loving kindness
Waiting at His mercy seat.

Remember, it's that secret place,
Where you can always find.....
Comfort and strength for the day,
And abundant peace of mind.

No one loves us like our Savior......
He gave His life on Calvary's tree,
Not only to bring us salvation,
But by His grace to set us free......

...free to enjoy all His blessings,
and freedom from bondage and slavery to sin...
there's no mountain top or valley,
where Jesus has not already been.

So when you're feeling sad and lonely,
And you just don't know what to do....
Get on your face before the throne,
Of the One who cares for you.

For there's no higher calling.....
Than to be a servant of the King.,
And no greater joy can ever be found....
Than being His servant can bring.

So, what is your calling.....
And are you happy, my friend?
If not ...come join the family....
And be His servant to the end.

2005

NO HIGHER CALLING *Continued...*

Psalms 34:22 The Lord redeems His servants; no one will be condemned who takes refuge in Him.

DON'T LIVE YOUR LIFE ON YOUR EMOTIONS

"Don't Live Your Life on Your Emotions" is a poem I wrote for me. I wrote it to remind myself of how deceptive our feelings and emotions can be. Not only are they ever changing but often the devil attacks us in that area. If we're not very careful we can think we're listening to the Lord and it's really just our own feelings, desires or emotions doing the whispering in our ear.

We must measure everything we think or believe with the solid, unchanging Word of God. That's the only way to keep from unwittingly making some bad choices and decisions.

We are much more likely to make good decisions and to think good thoughts, if we are in God's Word daily and in prayer without ceasing. And when we keep our sins confessed then we are in fellowship which allows the Holy Spirit the full and total freedom to direct our lives. The Holy Spirit will lead us into all truth and the truth sets us free. He will never lead us in the wrong direction, only we can do that.

Build your life on the solid rock, the rock of ages!

II Corinthians 10:3-6 For though we live in the world, we do not wage war as the world does. The weapons of our warfare are not carnal, but mighty through God to the pulling down of strongholds, the casting down of *imaginations*, and every high thing that exalts itself above the knowledge of God in our minds. Taking every thought into captivity to the obedience of Christ, and being ready to punish every act of disobedience, once your obedience is complete.

DON'T LIVE YOUR LIFE ON YOUR EMOTIONS

Don't live your life on your changing emotions,
But on the unchanging Word of God…..
For emotions can lead you down an unstable pathway,
Unfit for God's children to trod.

Emotions are always changing,
Just like the wind and the weather…..
But the Word of God never changes,
It's our solid foundation forever.

Feelings and emotions can be so fragile,
And we all need care and comfort now and then…..
Well, the Lord is the God of all comfort,
And He wants to bring peace to all men.

Living your life on your changing emotions,
Can only bring sorrow and pain…..
And when the up feelings are gone,
You're back down where you started from again.

So, don't build your house on the sinking sands of time,
But build it on the Word…the Rock of Ages…
For the Truth of God's Word is eternal,
And it has everlasting life between it's pages.

The fleeting treasures of this world,
Will never meet our need……
But the blessings in God's storehouse…..
Well, they'll always succeed.

My friend, trust the Lord…and His word… for everything,
Let Him be your All in All…..
And once you've found His all-sufficient comfort and grace,
Your feelings and emotions can never make you fall.

1985

John 1:1-2 In the beginning was the `Word, and the Word was with God, and the Word was God. He was with God in the beginning.

IT'S RAINING

"It's Raining" is a poem that was written during some times in East, Texas when I guess I could have felt forsaken by God. After all I had almost lost two of my children within 6 months of each other, and then we had lost our homes, vehicles, business and everything but the clothes on our backs. But strangely enough, I will always be able to look back on those years as some of the most blessed in my life. I always felt the nearness of His presence like never before, and it was a very special time. A time of growth in my relationship with the Lord.

The trials I went through only served to make me stronger in my walk with the Savior. I also found that on the other side of a tough circumstance a blessing is usually waiting. Trials are God's method of pruning us and you know what pruning does for plants? Well, it does the same thing for us.

God knows us better than we know ourselves, so He knows what it will take to make us into the fit vessel He wants us to be. So, friend, when you are going through a trial or testing time, just wait on the Lord, for He will bring you out on the other side of the circumstance, with a blessing, and usually in the end He even shows us why we had to go through a particular trial or test and what He was seeking to accomplish in our lives.

So dear one, when you're going through some tough times just remember it's not for nothing, it's for a purpose and the Lord will probably show you the reason very soon. Just trust Him for He loves you and only wants what is best for you.

Hebrews 12::11 No discipline for the present seems joyous, rather grievous, however, afterward it yields the peaceable fruit of righteousness unto those who are exercised by it.

IT'S RAINING

It's raining in my life,
the night is dark and lonely.....
when the thunder crashes and the lightning flashes,
help me to trust You, Lord, You only.

Times of testing rain upon me,
that at times I fear I can't endure.....
but I know it's raining for a purpose,
so in that I feel secure.

And though many a trial and affliction,
rain heavily down upon me.....
Your love and blessings,
through the rain I clearly see.

For no blossoms can ever bloom,
without the pouring showers of rain....
and no greater joy can ever be known,
than waits on the far side of pain.

Disappointments may rain fast,
on all my chosen plans and dreams.....
yet, in God's plans, our disappointments.....
are His appointments...so it seems.

When it's raining in my life,
It really isn't raining rain on me.....
It's raining showers of spiritual blessings,
That for a time I may not see.

For after the beating of the rain,
spiritual blossoms I find.....
that in a stormless, placid life,
could never be mine.

Blossoms of such beauty and fragrance,
that before I could not see.....
now I look forward to,
when God rains His rain on me.

IT'S RAINING Continued...

For it really isn't raining affliction,
it's raining joy, peace and love.....
compassion, patience and other spiritual gifts,
that only come from God above.

This world's ease and prosperity,
could never bring such treasure.....
as the Spirit forms within us,
with God's rain...in just the right measure.

1985

THE BUTTERFLY

The transformation of the caterpillar into a beautiful butterfly reminds me of the Lord taking a sinner and changing them into a saint. He takes something so ugly and makes it into something beautiful. He actually makes us into something He can use.

Just as the Butterfly is completely changed and no one would ever know or believe for that matter, that something so beautiful could possibly come from something so ugly, well, who would believe that our God could take a vile (extremely vile in some cases) sinner that the world feels like is a lost cause and turn their lives completely around?

Just as the Butterfly is a caterpillar that has been born again, so the saint is a born again sinner. It's so exciting to know what our God is capable of!

John 3:7 You must be born again.

John 3:3 Jesus replied, "I tell you the truth, no one can see the kingdom of God unless he is born again.

THE BUTTERFLY

When I see a butterfly,
leaving its' cocoon.....
I can't help but wonder,
what went on in that tiny room?

For the beautiful butterfly,
begins its' life as an ugly old worm.....
and as it crawls along....
I'm sure it must yearn.....

Yearn for its' wings,
for with wings it can soar....
no more need for crawling,
what worm could ask for more?

For not only are caterpillars,
ugly little things.....
but who wants to crawl,
when they can have wings?

It reminds me of our lives on earth,
and how in this body made of clay....
our spirit yearns within us,
for the sweet and blessed day.....

The day when we shall all be changed,
And our old bodies glorified.....
as we meet our Lord and Savior,
we'll realize we never died.

But we shall have brand new bodies,
leaving our old ragged tents far behind.....
trading them in at God's redemption store,
for the all-new heavenly kind.

And just as we know God takes a worm,
and makes a beautiful butterfly,
we know He can turn a sinner to a saint.....
in the twinkling of an eye..

1985

DADDY

When I wrote the poem "Daddy", I was hoping to let my Daddy know how much I loved and appreciated him. I guess I felt he was so special, for he was what the world calls a stepfather. (But of course to me he was Daddy.) And although the words stepfather or stepmother, at times today, can have a negative impact on our thinking, it really shouldn't be that way.

In my life, I felt so blessed to have my Daddy, for I had friends whose fathers couldn't compare to mine. Some had Daddies who were just not affectionate, some were down right mean, and one friend, Texanna, her father actually beat her mother and sometimes even her and her sister. I can remember at about 10 years old, spending the night and hiding under the covers when we could hear her father beating her mother and throwing her around the room. I was terrified, especially after being raised in a loving home.

Daddy always held down three jobs to give us not only our needs, but many of our wants. He wasn't extremely affectionate, but we always knew our Daddy loved us.

Although I know the Bible says that God hates divorce, I always felt like I was super blessed, for my real father left us and had another family, and even though they had lots of money and material things, he severely beat his wife and all 4 of his children. then he left them for a woman who had two grown children. So, I was always so thankful that my Momma was divorced, and that The Lord hand picked our wonderful Daddy. The Lord works in mysterious ways.

When my Daddy passed away, I thought to myself, if only I would have told him more frequently, how much he was loved and appreciated. But when I get up to heaven, we'll have all of eternity to talk and reminisce. I can only hope that he already knows how I felt about him and how thankful I was to our heavenly Father, for the special gift of my "Daddy".

Thank You Lord!

DADDY

I'm so glad out of all this world, Momma chose you to be my father…
and that when you found out she had me, you didn't say, "why bother?"

The Lord's plans are just so perfect, I'm so glad in mine He included you
…When Momma said, "I do", I said, "I do too".

I know many times it was probably hard, to put up with me when I was
young…and as I grew up you probably felt…my neck should have
definitely been rung.

The older I get the more I love you, and appreciate all that you've done,
And I'm just so thankful to know for sure….that you've accepted God's Son.

You gave us so much in love, time and money, I know you'll find it true
…that as God promises in His word, it will all come flooding back to you
(pressed down and running over)

You may not be rewarded, while living on this earth…..
but the rewards you'll receive in heaven, will be of far greater worth.

I could never pay you back, for all you've done, time and again….
I can only say, "I Love You"….and remind you now and then.

I don't get to see you much anymore, for sure… not enough anyway…
But Daddy, it's great to know….we'll be in heaven together ….someday.

Love you Daddy, God blessed me beyond measure
When He gave me my Daddy.

1986

LAWD, I BEEN A 'TRYIN

The poem LAWD is one of those poems that I really don't know why it came to me. But for some strange reason I kept picturing a very old, uneducated, black man, talking to the Lord. He had been doing the very best that he could to live the way he felt the Lord would want him to, and he probably lived under some very hard circumstances, yet He still wanted to please the Lord. I have always felt, the people who have suffered the most, and have been through the hardest times, due to their experiences, they have the most personal relationship with the Lord. I could just picture this wonderful, elderly gentleman baring his deepest feelings before his Savior and Lord. His simplicity was so sincere and innocent, in fact, probably the way the Lord would prefer that every believer would approach Him. He wants us to come as little children, in innocence and fully trusting.

Matthew 19:14 Jesus said, "Suffer the little children to come unto Me, for of such is the kingdom of Heaven.

LAWD, I BEEN A 'TRYIN

Lawd, I been a tryin' to do muh best,
To do right day by day.....
But when I comes to uh foak in da road,
Seems I always goes da wrong way.

I been a tryin' to do muh job,
An be good to da fokes I knows.....
But I jus can't seem to pleeze nobody,
Guess down here dat's a how it goes.

I been a lookin' forward to seein' Ya,
An to takin' dat chariot ride.....
One step ore da Jordan,
I be reached to da utter side.

I been longin' to see my family,
An da fokes who been gone befo.......
Lawd, I shur be a shoutin',
When I finely reach dat sho.

Hallelujah, I'll be a singin',
As I walks dem golden streets.....
An praizin' da Lawd amighty,
As I'z sittin' at Jesus'feet.

1985

Psalms 19:7 The law of the Lord is perfect, converting the soul: The testimony of the Lord is sure, making wise the simple.

Matt: 11:25 Jesus answered, "Oh, Father, Lord of heaven and Earth, Thou hast hidden these things from the wise and prudent and hast revealed them unto babes.

MY FRIEND, THIS IS MY PRAYER FOR YOU

When it comes to praying for our family and friends, I think it would be very easy, to pray for the Lord to shower down nothing but physical, spiritual, mental, emotional and financial blessings on them. But in reality, we need to be praying for the Lord to bring whatever it takes into their lives, in order to bring them closer to Him. For our loved ones and friends can have all the money in the world, all the material things they could ever desire, a brilliant and sound mind, and yet they could still be miserable. For the only real, true happiness this world has to offer comes from a right relationship with the Lord Jesus Christ and our Father God.

People can "have it all" as the saying goes, and be so unhappy, that they end up committing suicide, for all that this world has to offer can never truly satisfy the longing in a thirsty soul. Only Jesus can satisfy our soul.

So we need to pray, Father whatever it takes for my _____to draw closer to You and to have a right relationship with You, then please bring it to pass in his or her life.

No greater gift do we ever give anyone, than the opportunity for that person to give their life to Christ, and after that our prayers for their close walk with the Lord.

Romans 12:1-2 I beseech you therefore brethren, that you present your bodies as living sacrifices, holy and acceptable unto God, which is your reasonable service. And do not conform to this world, but be transformed by the renewing of your minds, so that you may prove what is that good, pleasing and perfect will of God is.

MY FRIEND, THIS IS MY PRAYER FOR YOU

Just enough joy, and then just enough pain…..
Just enough sunshine, and just enough rain.

Enough peace to sustain you, through the rough times ahead…..
The knowledge that truly, by His hand you are led.

Enough rest from your labors, to revive you again…..
Enough of His word, to sustain you within.
My friend this is my prayer for you.

Just enough heartache, with just enough loss…..
To make you keenly aware, of the cross and its' cost.

Enough of this world's trials, to give you a taste of His grace…..
Enough of His inner strength, to finish your race.

Just enough sorrow, and then just enough pain…..
To cause you to turn around and call on His name.

Enough wisdom of His word, so you'll truly believe…..
Then troubles and trials, so His grace you'll receive.
My friend, this is my prayer for you.

Enough of His mercy, and enough of His care…..
That you'll look forward to heaven, and His fellowship there

A life that shows His love, for all the world to see…..
Enough growth in grace and knowledge, to be what He wants you to be.

All the good things, that this life can hold…..
Not money, nor fame, not silver or gold…..

But a walk with the Lord, through this world and its' ways…..
The Holy Spirit to guide you, all of your days.
My friend, this is my prayer for you.

1985

115

I WAS MADE FOR YOU, LORD

If we are a believer in the Lord, Jesus Christ, then as the old song says, This World is Not Our Home. We are just passing through. We are on our way home, and we're excited about the thought of being with our Savior and our loved ones and friends who have gone before.

Whether in this world or the next, if you are a child of God, then you were made for and by Him for His service and His glory. That is probably one reason why nothing this world has to offer can ever really satisfy us. In this world, while we're here, only the things of the Lord really satisfy, and even though the things of this world can bring a moment of joy or happiness, it is always very fleeting.

When a saint of God is involved in the things of the Lord, they find a joy, peace and contentment that the things of this world will never be able to provide. We are in this world, but not of it.

We're homesick and yet we know that our Savior has a purpose for our being here for the time that He has allotted us. We should always seek His will and be ready to serve Him when He calls. He has a job for us to do while we are here, and when our job is over and our time for retirement is at hand we will be ready for His call to come home.

IICor.4:14-1 Because we know that the one who raised the Lord Jesus from the dead will also raise us with Jesus and present us with you in His presence. All this is for your benefit, so that the grace that is reaching more and more people may cause thanksgiving to overflow to the glory of God.

I WAS MADE FOR YOU, LORD

This world is not my home,
I'm just a stranger here…..
But as I'm passing through this way,
I feel Your presence near

Nothing this world has to offer,
can ever truly satisfy…….
like the thought of being with You,
in the sweet, sweet by and by.

The beauty of nature cannot satisfy,
Although it has a beauty all its' own…..
My spirit longs for You, Lord,
For You and You alone.

Every poem that I write,
Every song that I sing …..
I cannot begin to express,
The joy that they bring…..

For You… are my picture, my poem, my song,
the dreams that I dream are of You…..
Heaven is ever before me,
Forever I'll keep it in view.

I long to hear Your voice,
for no other sounds the same…..
my heart begins to rejoice,
at just the mention of Your name.

I consider the joys of life,
and none can ever compare…..
to the joy that heaven will bring,
and being in Your presence there.

For I was made for You, Lord,
and so, with You I long to be…..
but here on earth I must remain,
until You come for me.

Until that time I'll dream my dreams,
and with each poem and song…..
I'll feel a little closer,
to being home where I belong.

1985

Psalms 91: 14 "Because he loves me," says the Lord, "I will rescue him; I will protect him, for he acknowledges my name."

THIS IS NOT GOODBYE

Being in the cemetery and funeral home business for the last 21 years I have always asked the Lord to help me be a blessing to the grieving families that I have to deal with on a daily basis. I have prayed, that in some way I would be able to minister to them, comfort them in their time of loss, or if by chance they didn't know Jesus as their Savior, that the Lord would give me the privilege of leading them to a saving knowledge of the Lord Jesus Christ.

THIS IS NOT GOODBYE is one of several poems that the Lord has given me at a time when I felt a special burden for a particular family. Several years before I became the manager of White Chapel Memorial Gardens in Duluth, Georgia, the mother of the Irons family had gone to be with Jesus, and I had the privilege of meeting the family in October 2005 when their father went to join their mother in the presence of the Lord. When the family came in to make their father's arrangements, I immediately saw their love for the Lord and for one another. After they left my office, it's as if the Lord let me know, that I could lift their spirits and the spirits of many others, if I would let Him do it through me. So I said, "Here I am Father, use me in whatever way you choose." Soon the Lord gave me the words to the poem, THIS IS NOT GOODBYE.

If you have a loved one or friend, that has gone home to be with the Lord and this poem blesses you in some way, then may God the Father and our Lord Jesus Christ receive all the glory and honor and praise.

God Bless You Now and Forever More,

THIS IS NOT GOODBYE

My dear one I love you……..
And I know I'll miss you so…
And this old human flesh…….
Just doesn't want to let you go.

It's so hard to say goodbye….
To the dearest on earth to me..
But I know that you'll be waiting…
When I cross the Crystal Sea…

I know you'll save my place…
In our mansion up in glory…..
The one we always heard about….
In God's own special story……

So really this is not goodbye….
It's just I'll see you soon……
Way up in heaven's portals…
Just beyond the sun and moon.

You'll be waiting there to greet me…
As at last I step on shore…..
With the future we have waiting….
Who could ask for more?

Not only will we be together…..
With our family, friends and one another…
But just think…we'll be with Jesus….
And above Him…there is no other.!

He's the One, who ever so gently….
Will dry up all our tears…..
And remember up in heaven….
There'll be no more doubts or fears.

So, dear one for now……
I'll have those precious memories galore…..
And I'll keep them close to my heart…
Until we can make some more.

For we'll be living together ....
In our home up above.....
And dwelling forever......
In the light of God's love.

2005

NO ROOM

Sometimes, I think people who haven't accepted Christ as Savior, put it off because they honestly believe they don't have any more time left in their schedules for church and its' activities. They can't imagine how they could possibly give up their children's school and sports and ballet etc. activities. They don't realize, that they can accept Christ without giving up anything, but of course that's not to say, that at some time in the future their priorities won't change. Who knows? Right?

Then there are the believers, who have time for everything in their lives but the Lord. They have time for work, play, TV (of course) fishing and shopping, just about anything you can think of except for Jesus. But isn't it funny, how they want His help in times of trouble. And it is so sad that they don't realize the only thing in this world that can ever make them happy is the one thing for which they don't have time.

It's so easy, even for Christians, to let the cares and circumstances of this world crowd out our time with Jesus. And yet when we do, unfortunately we find everything in our lives, just seems to be out of kilter. Nothing seems to be going right, and everything seems to be going wrong.

But suddenly we hear a still small voice (the Holy Spirit), calling us back to the place where we belong, in the center of God's will, and when we're in the center of God's will we are always happier and more at peace than when we are in any other place.

So, let's make room for Jesus, regardless of what else has to go.

Jesus always has time and room for us. Praise His Name!

NO ROOM

My life was just so occupied,
with things I had to do…..
I often said to the Savior,
"Sorry, I have no room for You."

My time was just so busy,
with my own selfish ways…..
there was no room for Jesus,
in my nights or in my days.

I often felt an emptiness,
and skies weren't always blue…..
yet, I went right on saying,.
"Jesus, I have no room for you."

But by His precious Spirit,
at last I became aware…..
that there really is no life,
apart from being in His care.

For there's no good in me,
that I want the world to know…..
save the love of Jesus,
that He so wants me to show.

When our life is filled with self,
we can find no room for Him…..
but when we learn to die to self,
a whole new life will begin.

So, now in my life, instead of no room,
may there always be…..
plenty of room for Jesus,
and *no room for me.*

1986

Galatians 2:20 I am crucified with Christ, nevertheless I live, yet not I but Christ liveth in me and this life I now live, I live by the faith of the Son of Man, who loved me and gave Himself for me.

LET THEM REMEMBER

Friend, we may live a life that makes people compliment us, and to the world it may seem that we are a wonderful person. But what does Jesus think of us? To the world it may seem that we live a life of doing good to and for others, but only what's done for Christ will last. In fact we must learn to die to self and let Christ Himself live and work through us, so that all the praise and the glory belong to Him.

Many good works are done in the flesh and then we receive no heavenly rewards. Even a Christian can do all kinds of good things and when they do them with unconfessed sin in their lives (or we might say out of fellowship) then they receive no rewards whatsoever. that's one reason why it is so important to keep our sins confessed. I John 1:9 and Psalms 66:18 are both so important to a believer.

We of course, want our families and our friends to remember us, for the godly lives we lived while passing through this world. We could have all the money, fame and fortune this world has to offer and if we don't have a godly reputation what do we really have? We can leave our loved ones money and all our earthly goods, but if we didn't live a godly life before them, and we were not a godly example for others to see as well, then we have left our friends and loved ones nothing.

They can follow a godly example but money may be their downfall, if it didn't come with the godly example. So let's be more concerned with our witness than we are with our wealth. Let's ask ourselves if what we are doing is for us or for others? Are we doing the deed or are we letting Jesus work through us?

Friend, have your priorities in order and you won't have to worry about the legacy you leave. You'll be a blessing now and even after you're gone.

II Timothy 2:20-21 In a large house there are articles not only of gold and silver, but also of wood and clay; some are for noble purposes and some for ignoble. If a man cleanses himself from the latter, he will be an instrument for noble purposes, made holy, useful to the Master and prepared to do any good work.

LET THEM REMEMBER

I want no praise of men,
or their rewards for what I've done.....
I only hope and pray dear Lord,
that my life brought glory to Your Son.

And if I leave a reputation,
Among the folks I know....
Let it be that I served God,
While walking here below.

For the wisdom of all earthly things,
..... it's merely vanity.....
But knowing Christ as Savior,
Brings joy for all Eternity.

Not only in the eyes of others,
But in the eyes of my family as well....
(even though they were close enough,
to have seen me when I fell.)

I pray they'll remember no other vision,
That they may have seen in me.....
Than the one that says, "She loved the Lord,
For all the world to see."

Let the inheritance that I leave,
My children and loved ones when I go....
Be that of the Christ-like example,
That I so desire to show.

And when they sit and reminisce,
About the long ago.....
May they each one be able to say,
"You know...she loved God so".

September 1985

Gal.1:10 For do I now seek the favor of men, or of God? Or do I seek to please men? For if I yet pleased men, I should not be the servant of Christ.

RESISTING SATAN

Have you ever met people in your life that were just so hard to be around, that you wondered what they were living for? Well, there have been times in my own life, when I have had bosses that were so mean and ugly, and for no real reason, it's like they just enjoyed it. They felt like they were intimidating people by being loud and over-bearing.

One time when I had been transferred to Corpus Christi, Texas as the area manager for Equity Corporation (ECI); the owner of the company was a godly Christian, and we never had drinking or smoking in the manager's meetings and no vulgar language or profanity. We were the Fourth largest cemetery and funeral home company in the United States, when Jon(one of the main owners) decided to sell his portion of the company and go into fulltime Christian Service. Well, from the time he sold out, the man that took over running the company was the complete opposite of Jon.

Even though my location where I officed in my area, and my area itself were always number 1 or 2 in the company, this man talked to me like dirt and even the other managers and my secretaries and sales people couldn't believe it. They would come to me and say, "Carolyn, why in the world does he talk to you that way?" And all I could say was, I Don't know, and I didn't. It was so bad at one manager's meeting that driving back to Corpus Christi, I cried nearly all the way. I kept on asking the Lord, why this was happening to me. Suddenly, it was like the Lord spoke to me and said, "Carolyn, you don't know what this man may have gone through or may be going through in his own life." So I prayed for wisdom and asked the Lord to please, show me what to do. The next day I went to the Bible Book Store and I got a little card with an old shepherd on the front with a long white beard, and he was leaning over a cliff pulling a little lamb up with the crook in his staff and it said, "it pays to have friends in high places." I wrote a little note in the card and mailed it. Immediately, I got a nice card back from him saying, "You'll never know what that card meant to me and it came at just the right time." I couldn't believe it.

From that time on until I left the company, he was the nicest person in the world to me and when I went to another company, he would periodically call to see how I was doing. Later we worked together again for the same company and he would call me on a regular basis to see how I was or just to congratulate me for having a good week or month of sales.

Through this experience so many lives were touched, for so many people saw the way the Lord gave me the grace to respond when he was so ugly, and then after three years of prayer, the incredible changes that took place in our relationship and even until today I consider Bill a personal friend and can talk to him about the Lord, or anything else for that matter. God is so faithful and so good. NEVER GIVE UP ON ANYONE!!!

God never gives up on us, we should never give up on anyone else.

RESISTING SATAN

The cruel tongues of men,
Can sting us when they hurl.....
Cutting words meant to put,
Our lives into a whirl.

Satan uses the tongues of men,
And tries his best to get us down.....
He makes every effort,
To turn our smile into a frown.

But when we realize,
You just can't hurt the dead...
When Satan hurls his evil darts,
We won't cry...we'll laugh instead.

For as children of God we're dead to sin,
Old things have passed away.
Satan is banned from coming in...
For Christ lives here to stay.

Now that I am finally dead...
And Jesus Christ lives in me,
By His strength...not mine,
Satan will quickly flee.

So when people try to hurt us,
By the ugly things they do....
Remember Jesus is your protector,
So they can't get the best of you.

In fact, look at them through Jesus' eyes,
And forgive them where they stand.....
They really need some love and care,
So reach out and offer a hand.

By reaching out to those who are lost,
We can snatch them from the fire....
And when the old devil tries to deceive us,
We'll just tell him he's a liar.

1985

RESISTING SATAN Continued...

John 8:44 You belong to your father, the devil, and you want to carry out your father's desire, he was a murderer from the beginning, not holding to the truth, for there is no truth in him. When he lies he speaks his native language, for he is a liar and the father of lies.

OUR SECRET

Have you noticed, that even as a believer, we sometimes fall into the judging and criticizing mode? In fact, when we are out of fellowship it is so easy to see the sins and faults of others that it is funny. I say funny, because we can so easily see the other brother or sister's sin but we often have such a hard time seeing our own. Why can't we hear the voice of the Holy Spirit trying to get us to concern ourselves with the log in our own eye instead of the splinter in our brothers'.

Just as scripture says, He that seeks love covers the transgression, but he that repeats a matter separates friends. It also says, love covers a multitude of sins. God our wonderful Father is so gracious and loving to us, that He is very gentle most of the time about pointing out our sins to us, but then there are times that He really has to knock us in the head in order to get our attention. He keeps on until He makes us aware of any sin that has taken hold in our lives.

Next to our salvation experience the second most important thing that a believer will ever learn is to keep their sins confessed (I John 1:9) because when we have unconfessed sin in our lives God doesn't hear our prayers(Psalms 66:18) and it keeps us out of fellowship. When a believer is out of fellowship they can really be a pain to be around, but the minute we confess our sins we are immediately back in fellowship with the Lord, and usually that makes us much easier to get along with. I sometimes like to say, rebound and keep moving. Confess your sin and then forget it and keep on serving our Father.

Let's concentrate on having victory over our own sins and weaknesses, and let the Lord take care of making others aware of theirs.

James 4:12 who are you to judge your neighbor?

Romans 2:16 this will take place on the day when God will judge men's secrets through Jesus Christ.

Romans 14:10 why do you judge your brothers? Or why do you look down on your brother? For we will all stand before God's judgment seat.

OUR SECRET

There's a little secret, Lord……
Kept by You and me,
About the ugliness within……
That others may not see.

I'm so glad that You won't tell…..
Our secret to the world,
For if they really knew the truth,
Well, stones at me they'd hurl.

For each one of us has a way,
Of seeing another's sin…..
But we're so busy looking about,
We forget to look within.

If everyone worried about their own sins…..
And not the sins of others,
Then we'd feel less like judges…..
And a little more like brothers.

Help me to see myself…..
As You see me, Father,
Then about the sins of others……
Don't let me ever bother.

Thank you, for keeping our secret,
And not telling a single soul,
They only know me in part…..
But You know the whole.

Help me to be inside and out….
Just what You want me to be,
And then there won't be any secrets,
That we'll have to keep about me.

1985

131

CAN YOU PRAISE HIM?

There are times in our lives, that from the world's perspective, we should just give up or give in. Times when it seems like, maybe God doesn't *really* know how much we can bear. Surely, He has me confused with someone else.

Friend, if you can find it within yourself, to start praising the Lord, many times you can praise the hurt away. You can't continue to praise the Lord and stay down at the same time. Phil.4: 4-9 says, Rejoice in the Lord always, again I say rejoice! Let your gentleness be known unto all men. The Lord is near. Do not be anxious about anything, but in everything, by prayer and supplication, with thanksgiving let your request be made known unto God. And the peace of God, which passes all understanding, will guard your hearts and minds in Christ Jesus. Finally, brothers, whatever is true, whatever is noble, whatever is right, whatever is pure, whatever is lovely, whatever is of good report, if anything is excellent or praiseworthy-think about such things. Whatever you have learned or received or heard or seen in me do and the God of Peace will be with you.

We have so much to be thankful for, that we can always find something for which to praise the Lord.. And when you push out the negative and replace it with the positive, it always changes your perspective. There is no room for both good and evil, negative and positive. It's up to you which one you allow to control and influence your life. When Jesus is on the throne, it's much easier to walk in the Spirit, in fact, when you keep your sins confessed and walk in the Spirit, you really can't keep from praising the Lord.

Regardless of our circumstances, whether they are bleak or blessed, we can praise Him. And somehow, praise has a way of changing our outlook on things. It makes the darkness lighter and the day brighter. It brings joy out of sorrow and peace out of panic. So don't forget to praise Him when you're happy, praise Him when you're sad, when feeling sick or when feeling well, day and night, driving down the road or sitting in your house PRAISE THE LORD!

God is good all the time!

CAN YOU PRAISE HIM?

Can you praise Him through the testing time…
Can you praise Him through the trial?
When your world is crashing about you….
Can you praise Him all the while?

Can you trust Him through your grief,
And through the times so hard to bear?
When your heart is filled with sorrow,
Can you feel you're in His care?

Do you love Him more than life….
Do you love Him more each day?
No matter how rough or hard your journey..
Will you love Him all the way?

Have you surrendered your all to Jesus….
Have you surrendered your life and loved ones dear?
Or are you holding something back…
Because your heart is filled with fear?

Do you spend time in His Word….
Do you spend time with Him in prayer?
Do you find yourself so busy…..
That your time with Him is rare?

Are you thankful in your heart….
And even clear down in your soul…
That you can go to Jesus…
And give Him full…complete control?

Praise Him and Trust Him….
And love Him more each day…..
Surrender your all to the Master….
And let Him show you the way.

The way to peace and joy....
To love that has no end…..
Out of the crowd…out of this world….
Into the arms of your dearest Friend.

1985

Psalms 34:1 His praise will always be on my lips.

JESUS I LOVE YOU

Friend, have you ever felt like you were just going to burst with joy and thankfulness? Even though it may seem that all around you the world is in chaos and there are storms surrounding you on every side. It may seem like the darkest hour that you have ever been through and yet, for some strange reason, there are times in the midst of the storms of life, that you feel so thankful that you have Jesus, and that He loves you and cares about what you are going through.

You may also find there are times, that you are rejoicing and yet you find yourself in tears, when you think of all He did for you when He suffered and died on Calvary's cross. It was on one of those days, that this poem, JESUS I LOVE YOU, came to me, and it barely reflects the real extent of the joy we feel in our hearts, for truly there are no words to express how we feel, about our wonderful Lord and Savior and ALL that He is TO us and ALL that He has done FOR us.

Dear one, may you experience that unspeakable joy, happiness and peace of mind in your life today. It can only come into your life if you have trusted Jesus Christ as your personal Lord and Savior. If you haven't done that, please, don't delay but ask Him into your life today.

Ps. 18:1-2 I love You, Lord, You are my strength. The Lord is my Rock, my Fortress and my Savior; My God is my rock, in whom I find protection. He is my shield, the strength of my salvation, and my stronghold.

JESUS I LOVE YOU

Jesus, I love you so much
All because you care
And life and all its dreams….
Wouldn't matter if you weren't there.

You're the lily of the valley,
The peace within my soul…
The joy of life forever
The sweetest story ever told.

Not because of who I am…
But because you always care.
Not because I'm always faithful…
But because you're always there.

You make life worth living,
And You give me joy through out the day…
When I'm lost and lonely,
You help me find my way.

You're the God of second chances,
You forgive me for all my sin…..
And when I lay life at your feet
You give me peace within.

You're the Alpha and the Omega,
You're the beginning and the end.
My strong hold and high tower,
My dearest and best friend.

Let me share your mercy and love,
With people all around…..
And let the lost and lonely know,
How Your grace and love abound.

You're my shield in the time of trouble,
My shelter in the time of storm…..
And in my darkest hours,
You keep me safe from harm.

JESUS I LOVE YOU Continued...

Jesus, I love you,
What more can I say……
The debt I truly owe You,
I could never repay.

The river of Your love is never ending,
Its' depth we cannot comprehend…..
Even when we're up in Heaven,
It's flow will never end.

2005

LET US BE THANKFUL

God is so good to us. He provides for all our needs while we're living here on earth, but the greatest provision He ever made for us, was when He provided the total and complete, onetime sacrifice for our sins. He loved us so much that He sent His own beloved Son to die in our place. Are we thankful in Word only, or in word and in deed?

Are we thankful not only for our salvation, but for everything that our Father has provided for us. Do we ever stop and think about all He has provided? Our friends and loved ones, the beauty of nature, our jobs, our homes, our transportation, living in America, our health, and the list goes on and on of the things and people that the Lord has brought into our lives to bless us, all because He loves us. What an awesome God we have!

Let's let our Father know on a regular basis, how truly appreciative we are. We ourselves like to hear from our friends and loved ones when we've done something to bless them, in fact if we don't hear something from them, then we are sometimes hurt or offended and whatever we have done, it can't compare to what our Lord has done for us. How does He feel about such ungrateful children?

Let us shower Him with praise and thanksgiving on a daily basis, and that way we'll never forget all His wonderful benefits and blessings.

Let's not just say, Father, thank You for all Your blessings, but let's actually meditate on all that He has done for us and hopefully it will cause us to be truly thankful.

Psalm 95:1-2 Come, let us sing for joy to the Lord; let us shout aloud to the Rock of our salvation. Let us come before Him with thanksgiving and extol Him with music and song.

Psalm 100:4-5 Enter His gates with thanksgiving and His courts with praise; give thanks to Him and praise His name. For the Lord is good and His love endures forever; His faithfulness continues through all generations.

LET US BE THANKFUL

Let us thank our Father God,
That He loved us enough…..
To send His one and only Son to die,
For each one of us.

Let us remember that precious Baby,
That He was born to die on the tree…..
A terrible death…..on a cruel cross,
To save sinners like you and me.

Let us be thankful,
Our God loved us so…..
And because of that love,
He stooped so low…..

…..to take off His crown,
and to leave heaven above…..
to die for lost sinners,
all because of His love.

Let us thank Him for our loved ones,
We hold so very dear…..
For they are always in our hearts,
Whether they are far or near.

Then let us thank our loving Father,
For the beauty all around…..
And that even more awaits,
In that home where we're bound.

Let us have an attitude of gratitude,
In the good times and the bad…..
And let us be rejoicing,
When we're happy or we're sad.

For we have a loving Father,
Who graciously takes care of His own…..
And we'll always be His children… even when we are grown.

LET US BE THANKFUL Continued...

So let us always be thankful,
For all our Father's done…..
And for all of His wonderful blessings,
Starting with His own dear Son.

Thank you Father!

2005

Phil 4:6 Be anxious for nothing, but in everything through prayer and WITH THANKSGIVING let your request be made known unto God and the Peace of God, which passes all understanding, will keep your hearts and minds through Christ Jesus.

LETTING GO

Letting Go is a poem that I wrote at a time when life had become very fragile. Both of my children had almost gone home to be with the Lord that same year, about six months apart. We had also lost everything financially during that same period of time. I guess because of those events occurring so close together, I had gotten to where I was holding onto my children, loved ones and friends too tightly and the Lord wanted me to let go and let Him have them.

It's funny that I had no problem giving Him all our material possessions, and not ever taking them back. I guess they had lost all of their importance to me, when I almost lost Debbie and Mark. The Lord allowing me to keep my children made material things so insignificant and unimportant.

The Lord knows that holding on to anything too tightly, causes us to be worrying constantly about losing that person, or with some people it can be worrying about losing some material thing. Either way when we don't give everything to God we live in fear of losing whatever we are holding on to, and we believe we can't make it without that person or that thing. People have actually committed suicide after a divorce or after losing their home to bankruptcy, or because of financial reversals.

Besides, friend, what better place can our loved ones and friends be, than In God's love and care? So let go and let God have it all and then rest in His love, knowing that He not only wants what is best for you but for them as well.

Proverbs 3:5-6 Trust in the Lord with all your heart and lean not on your own understanding. In all your ways acknowledge Him and He will direct your paths.

LETTING GO

Help me, Father, to let go, of all that I hold dear…..
Trusting all to Your loving care and letting go of fear.

Fear and doubt and worry, only cause us to feel lowdown….
While trusting frees God's children…to turn their lives around.

Fear and doubt are like a vise, with an ever-tightening grip…..
It's like walking on a tightrope, and you're just about to slip.

It's time to let go of loved ones, held so tightly… …we thought for their
own good, but oftentimes we've held them more tightly than we should.

In some way we must feel, by letting them go they'll run away…..
But with their new found freedom, comes a strange desire to stay.

Do we trust our heavenly Father, enough to entrust them to His care,
Or do we hold them even tighter and say, "Let go? I wouldn't dare!"

But by holding on too tightly, we may crush a fragile soul…..
That in freedom might have soared, to some divinely appointed goal.

So although the hurt may seem at times, almost too great to bear…..
We'll always find a blessing, when at last we learn to share.

For God's thoughts and ways are higher, than mine could ever be…..
And my Father always wants what's best, for my loved ones and for me.

1985

Hebrews 2:13 I will put my trust in Him

**I Cor. 13:7 Love always protects, always trusts Always hopes, always
perseveres.**

LOVE THE UNLOVELY

Have you ever felt like you were a pretty loving person, because you love God, your family, the people at church your friends and neighbors and your co-workers? Many people consider themselves to be loving people because they are family oriented and they are active in their church. But you know what friend, if we can't love that stinky vagrant off the street unconditionally, or that prisoner who just got out of prison for their crimes, then we can't be pleasing to God the Father.

God our Father says to love all men the same. LOVE THE UNLOVELY, the one who doesn't dress, walk, talk, or act the same way we do. You know you might open your wallet and give them some money, but would you give them a roof over their heads?

Years ago the Lord blessed me so much by giving me the privilege of being in the prison ministry. I have been to prisons all over the country and Mexico. Well, several times over the years, inmates getting out and needing a place to stay, have come to live in our home for extended periods of time. It has up to this point, always been a great blessing and I wouldn't trade the experiences we've had and the relationships we've made, because of my dear loving God, allowing me to go to the prisons. Loving the unlovely takes a conscious decision. I always hated tattoos, so now, I don't really notice them and try not to judge a man or woman because of them. In fact, maybe to teach me a lesson, two of my grandsons who are in the Navy ended up getting tattoos, and I was disappointed but the Lord has helped me get over it and be thankful that they are such fine young men. Besides, I don't think God is that concerned with tattoos, I think He's more concerned with the heart.

If for some reason you don't feel that you can love the unlovely, all you have to do is ask the Lord to do it through you. He already loves them, and if you let Him, He will fill you up and love them for you. So once you empty yourself out and let the Lord fill you up and love through you, anytime that you find yourself unable to love the unlovely, then you will know it's because you have gotten out of fellowship and you have become filled with self again. For only God can do for us, what we can't do ourselves.

James 2:1-3 As believers in the Lord Jesus Christ, don't show favoritism. If a man comes into your meeting wearing a gold ring and fine clothes, and a poor man in shabby clothes also comes in, if you show special attention to the man wearing fine clothes, have you not discriminated?

LOVE THE UNLOVELY

It's easy to love those who love us,
It's easy to care for those who care.....
But the ones who need love the most,
With them we find love hard to share.

Do we find it hard to love the unlovely,
The one who… happens to rub us the wrong way?
What about the fellow… who's sullen and mean,
And 'never' has a nice thing to say?

Many times we know, our attitude is wrong,
It's really not what it should be.
So, we ask the Lord, "What's the matter?"
When He says, "It's you!" we say, Me?"

Now… we try to fool ourselves,
And say, "surely I must have misunderstood".
I go to church… and read my Bible.....
And I treat 'everybody', pretty good!

Soon we get all out of sorts,
And with our Savior…we just have to disagree….
So, finally, in desperation we turn to Him,
And say, "What do I have to do…if it's me?"

When He said, "You must love the unlovely".
It's the only way out of your despair.
Then I grew uglier than ever….
Whatever He says…I don't care!

The struggle within me, seemed to last forever.....
Faster and faster I was going down hill.
Jesus tenderly whispered, "Can't you love them for My sake?"
At last I said, "yes, Lord, I will".

At once peace filled my sin hardened heart,
And I felt a new joy surge within.....
I yielded my will to the Master,
And He wrought love from my sin.

It's never the unlovely one…..
Who causes our despair,
It's the precious Holy Spirit convicting us,
Of our lack of genuine love and care

Listen to the Holy Spirit, Dear One!

1986

MEME

MeMe was my precious grandmother, and she and my grandfather (from the time my brother and I were babies) were both the most wonderful, loving grandparents in the world. With all they did for us, there was never any question that we were their life.

We felt so blessed that God had given us our MeMe and Poppy. Nobody else could possibly have had the wonderful summers, and holidays that we had down in Brownsville, Texas at their house. Truly, the happiest days of my childhood were spent with MeMe and Poppy.

Later in life when I had a family of my own, and we were living in East, Texas and the economy had gotten so bad in Texas in the mid eighties, that we had gone bankrupt and lost our business, homes and vehicles. I had gone to work at Texicolors, Inc. and we were barely scraping by, when MeMe's birthday came, and I didn't even have the money for a card or for a stamp, but the Lord was so gracious, that He gave me my first poem I had ever written, and I asked my boss if I could have a stamp to mail it.

The minute MeMe received the home-made card, she called me crying and said that the card meant by far more than any store bought card she had ever had. And from that time forth the Lord started giving me poems on every subject and of every kind. I can only pray that they glorify Him in someway, and that someone's heart is blessed or their spirit is encouraged by reading some of them. If so, then I of all people am most blessed.

MEME

Little pink tongue...
Peeks from behind – white teeth,
When she laughs.

Eyes sparkle....
And kinda squench-up,
When she laughs.

Tears roll down soft, wrinkled cheeks....
When she cries or....
When she laughs.

The Lord has placed...
A crown of silver on her head,
And the angels smile...
When she laughs.

Joy swells in the hearts...
Of those around her....
Family, friends and pets,
When she laughs.

Thank you, Father...
That my heart rejoices,
When I think about her ....
And when she laughs.

She's my MeMe.....
And I love her,
All the time, but especially....
When she laughs.

There will never, ever be another MeMe

Love,   Carolyn

1985

WHAT IS OUR MOTIVE?

Dear one, it is wonderful to see Christians serving the Lord. Not just being Pastors and missionaries but Christians serving God right where they are. But when we are serving God, are we doing it for His glory or for ours? Sometimes people enjoy hearing the praises of men and they forget who it is that they are really serving.

We as Christians are blessed to have the opportunity to serve God, and we must never forget that in any good deed that we do, we should only be doing it for God to receive the praise and the glory, because God is actually doing that good deed through us, and He merely allowed us the privilege of being the vessel that He chose to use to accomplish His purpose.

We should never seek praise for ourselves, but there is certainly nothing wrong after having an opportunity to serve God, for a Christian to feel joyful at heart for God having chosen him or her for that particular means of serving.

There is no greater joy than to used by God. And our only goal should be, that when we get to heaven we hear God say, "Well done thou good and faithful servant". The praise of men can be shallow and deceitful, but the praise of God will last for all eternity.

Christians should never seek a pat on the back from the world and they certainly should never toot their own horn, I believe they will lose all their rewards in heaven in either instance. So, please, be satisfied with the wonderful privilege of serving the King of Kings and the Lord of Lords and forget about ever trying to please men. For when you please God, usually men will also be pleased.

WHAT IS OUR MOTIVE

What is our motive, when we seek to be loved?
Do we desire glory for ourselves, or for the Lord above?

Do our hearts seek to please men, in order to gain their praise?
Do we try to toot our own horn…or a heavenly banner raise?

Do we do for others, trying to win their approval?
Or seek out that lost and lonely one…because they are needful?

Why, do we by our good deeds, seek a pat on the back?
If not from someone else, we'll pat our own in fact!

We should always examine, the intents of our hearts,
To make sure we don't (by accident?)…..
Have the cart before the horse.

For pleasing God should always come, before pleasing men.
Our putting others first…that always pleases Him.

Whatever is done in the Spirit…..won't come out smelling like smoke….
But if everything's done in the flesh,…when they pass out rewards we'll be
broke.

For deeds done in the flesh, will soon be burned away…..
And some will stand…with no rewards… on that judgment day.

Thank God, that knowing Jesus…..makes our salvation sure….
And not the motives of our hearts, for they're not always pure.

1989

II Corinthians 5:9 So we make it our goal to please Him.

MY BOSS

"My Boss" is a poem that I wrote during the period of time when we had lost everything financially and I had to go to work. There weren't many jobs in the little town where we lived and the Lord was so good to me and He led me to a job making a pretty good hourly wage for a small town in East, Texas in the 1980's. I took a job in Jacksonville as the office manager for Texicolors, Inc., a company that made dyes for plastics.

I had a boss that I really liked and the owner of the company fired the man, who was doing a great job, simply due to what the owner called a personality conflict. Then the next day he brought in one of his personal friends to take the position.

Well, the new boss was so different from the old one, different in everyway. The first one went to church, didn't smoke or drink or cuss and the new boss was the complete opposite. Back in those days of my Christianity, I foolishly thought, oh, no, this is just going to be horrible and I had already made up my mind that I wasn't going to like my new boss. But God is so good and He quickly let me know that I had no business prejudging any of His children. And of course my Father proved me wrong.

I found that just because a person may smoke, drink or even cuss a little it doesn't mean that they are not a Christian or that God has not put them into your life for a purpose. I may not do what that person does, but I have no room to judge another when I am not perfect myself. There may be things I do or thoughts that I think that are more displeasing to the Lord than smoking, drinking or cussing.

My new boss turned out to be a kind, thoughtful person that I was glad I had the opportunity to get to know. Life would be so boring if we were all exactly the same. And we are all in a different place in our walk with the Lord. Thank God for His patience with us.

God is good all the time!

Praise His Name!

Carolyn

MY BOSS

He surprised me that old fella, I had decided I wouldn't like...
He smoked and drank and then, by George, he even cussed a mite.

But I'm so glad the Lord said, "Hey, Carolyn, who are you...
To quickly judge My children, before they're in full view?"

You don't know start from finish – so love all men the same.
I use each one in a unique way...to bring glory to My name.

His name was Leo Hicks...he came upon the scene, and for
Some unexplained reason, I thought he might be mean.

But to my surprise and joy...the Lord showed me I had erred...
He turned out to be a thoughtful soul and about us all he cared.

To have a boss is one thing, a good one something else.
The Bible says obey them(good or bad), and not to think of self.

The Lord chooses those who cross our path, in one way or another.
Each will leave their imprint...in a certain color.

The colors fit and blend together, to make a perfect plan...
A plan marked out by God alone, for each and every man.

Some colors may seem harsh...others seem more soothing,
But each one is just perfect, if we let God do the choosing.

So, Lord, help me not to judge men ever, not just ahead of time.
For in my haste, I might misjudge a good, good friend of mine.

1986

Hebrews 13:17 Obey your leaders and submit to their authority. They keep watch over you as men who must give an account. Obey them so that their work will be a joy, not a burden, for that would be of no advantage to you.

PEAKS AND VALLEYS

Friend have you ever felt like everything has been going right (and it makes you feel so good), and you pray that things will remain that way and then all of a sudden the bottom drops out and absolutely everything that can go wrong does? Finally, you think nothing else can possibly go wrong, and sure enough it does.

My poems STORMS and PEAKS AND VALLEYS came to me just when everything in my life seemed to be falling apart. My son Mark had been shot by his best friend Matt, by accident. They came in from hunting, and when they went upstairs to listen to the stereo Matt didn't unloaded his gun like he should have, and when he went to hand it to Mark to put it on the dresser, it went off and Mark was hit in the stomach with a 22 magnum hollow point bullet, which is an Exploding shell that bursts into fragments upon impact.

At the hospital the doctor said the xrays showed that the bullet fragments had hit most of his vital organs, and that he would be in surgery about 3–5 hours. During the time that Mark was in surgery I didn't cry a tear, which was very strange, for I had always been the type to cry if I was happy, sad, or for the least little thing, but it was as if I could literally feel the Lord, carrying me above the circumstance. He continually brought scriptures to mind that I had memorized over the years; and I kept visualizing Abraham putting Isaac on the altar, and he was willing to sacrifice him there. Would I be willing? I could only say, "Lord, You, know my heart and my heart cries out, please, spare my son, yet Father I know whatever Your will is, You are somehow going to see us through this. Praise the Lord! He chose to let my son live, even though he was in the hospital 3 weeks, and then we almost lost our daughter Debbie 6 months later and she was in the hospital 4 days.

Isn't it amazing, that you can have insurance galore, and never have a claim on it, now just when we needed it most, we found out our company secretary, had been paying what bills she could with the money that had been coming in, and she had let the insurance lapse. We had thousands of dollars in medical bills and no money and no insurance.

The economy had gotten so bad in Texas in the early 1980s, that we ended up a few months after nearly losing Mark and Debbie, losing everything we had but the clothes on our backs. We gave our pastor and his wife 3 bedrooms, 1 living and 1 dining area of furniture for we couldn't even afford a storage unit. When we were forced to move out of our 5 bedroom house into a tiny 2 bedroom apartment. I was so blessed to be able to have a Bible Study with 32 teenagers I would never have met, if we had not been forced to move into the apartment. It ended up being one of the happiest times of my life.

After losing everything materially, and God sparing my children, I asked the Lord never to allow me to be attached to worldly things. So I have learned to abase and to abound and to say blessed be the name of the Lord.

I also learned that our disappointments are God's appointments, and that whether we are on the mountaintop or down in the valley, Jesus is there, and wherever we are with Him THAT'S DIVINE! He's in the midst of the fiercest storm and He's the light in the darkest night. He has been and always will be with us, and that as the old song says, makes every day with Jesus sweeter than the day before.

Friend He loves you right where you are, and whatever you are going through He will see you through. Trust Him!

PEAKS AND VALLEYS

In this life of ups and downs......
Often times we long to stay.....
High atop the mountain......
For forever and a day......

The view is so far-reaching......
Faith comes easily so it seems.....
And we long to stay on top.....
Where it's almost like a dream.

When we're up on the mountain.....
The physical world seems to dim...
And our spiritual sight and power...
Suddenly overflow their brim.

Then...alas, like a vapor....
The mountaintop experience fades away...
And we long to clutch it tightly....
Oh, please, let it stay.

But...suddenly it's gone....
Leaving only a vivid memory in it's place...
And once again we find ourselves....
Back in the rat race.

Just remember...it's in the everyday rat race....
Down in the valley once again....
That somehow God puts spiritual character....
Back into the lives of men.

The view from the top of the mountain....
Appeals very well to our sight.....
Yet, while walking through the valley....
We walk by FAITH and by His might.

Jesus is as real in our daily routine.....
As at the peak of our spiritual high.....
So...when walking through the valley...just trust...
There's really no need to ask, why?

Friend, walking close to our Savior…
Through the valley dark and deep….
Can yield a far greater blessing ….
Than the highest mountain peak.

1986

TAKE MY LIFE AND USE IT

Child of God, the unbeliever has an excuse, but the child of God, has no excuse for living his life out of the will of his Father. When God created us, He created us to have fellowship with Him, and to glorify Him. He didn't create man, just to live his own life and to do his own thing. Yet, God the Father made us with a freewill. He didn't want a bunch of robots, that He made to love and serve Him.

Would it mean anything to us if we created a robot, that looked and acted exactly like a person. It was beautiful, acted loving and attentive and was very intelligent. And no one knew it was a robot but we ourselves. We knew that we had programmed it to say all the sweet, loving things, and to perform all the thoughtful deeds. It just wouldn't mean anything to us because we knew we had created it to say and do these things.

God wanted us to choose to love Him from our own freewill. He does everything trying to win our love and affection, just as we do with someone we love. Yet most of the time we choose to do our own thing and only give God the leftovers of our time and attention. Oh, we'll turn to Him in times of need, hardship or sorrow; but many Christians don't have time for the Lord (in their everyday routine) on a regular basis. They believe in Him and claim that they love Him, but is that what we would really call love?

Most people never find out, that being close to the Lord and letting Him use you in His service, are the greatest blessings we will ever have. Nothing the world has to offer can ever compare to the joy and happiness found in the service of the King of Kings and Lord of Lords. Even though the flesh is weak and wants to lean toward the things of this world, we should say, "Father, whatever it takes to get me to surrender to You and Your will, then bring it into my life." If we knew the blessings that come from being obedient, I believe we would be more willingly obedient children.

Father, take us and make us into what You want us to be, even if it has to be against our will. And we'll thank You for it.

Matthew 26:41 The spirit is willing but the flesh is weak.

TAKE MY LIFE AND USE IT

Take my life and use it, Lord,
in Your own special way…...
just to be a blessing,
and to brighten someone's day

Please, Lord let it count,
for something that glorifies Your name…..
and if I hold back in any way,
well, use it just the same.

You have my permission,
to take full, complete control…..
(even against my resistance),
of body, mind and soul.

For I know I have no righteousness,
that I can call my own…..
and any good that's found in me,
comes from You and You alone.

Father, at times I may resist,
doing Your perfect will…..
but if it takes the chastening rod,
then keep on chastening still.

For in my heart I know,
the only peace and joy I'll find…..
is when I'm completely yielded to You,
In my heart, my soul, and mind.

I know without a doubt,
that true peace and joy abound…..
only in the center of Your will,
where Your grace and love are found.

The flesh is oh, so weak,
but the spirit yearns to obey…..
so, Father, let Your will be mine…..
take my hand and lead the way.

1985

THE LITTLE THORNY BRIAR

The Little Thorny Briar is a poem that I wrote, when I was thinking about how the Lord takes something as insignificant as a sinner (such as I) and He can, if we let Him, make something useful to Himself and to His service.

Just as He took the Little Thorny Briar, and He grafted something into it, in order to make it beautiful, and to satisfy the longings of the Little Thorny Briar; God can and will take us and graft in our new nature through the salvation experience, and then He seals us with His Holy Spirit.

You know, dear saint of God, before we knew Christ as our Savior, there was only worldly good in us, and worldly good is no good at all. And even after we accept Christ, when we live our lives out of fellowship, we might do some good works, but we will lose our rewards.(not our salvation). Only works done in the power of the Holy Spirit, earn us any rewards.

Once we accept Jesus, when God the Father looks at us, He looks at us through Christ's blood. Just as the little Thorny Briar became the beautiful Briar Rose, due to a little surgery, so we become beautiful in the eyes of God when we have our spiritual surgery. In fact during surgery the old man dies and the new man becomes alive in Christ.

Friend, if you haven't been made new, please don't delay and let Jesus make a new person out of you today!

God Bless You!

Galatians 5:17 Therefore if anyone is in Christ, he is a new creation; the old has gone, the new has come!

THE LITTLE THORNY BRIAR

The little Thorny Briar.....
Feeling sorry for itself,
Thought...all the pretty blooms.....
Why couldn't I be one myself?

Briars are good for nothing,
They're worthless as can be.....
Just growing in a ditch,
Scratchy and scraggily, that's me!

Then one day along came a gardener,
And dug the little briar up.....
Put him in his garden,
With roses, tulips and buttercups.

The little thorny briar thought.....
He doesn't know me or he wouldn't waste his time,
Surely he must realize.....
No sweet blossoms are mine.

But the gardener said, "If I can't get any good out...
Then I'll just put some in".
And he quickly made a slit,
In the little briar's skin.

Inside the slit he put a little bud...
And fastened it tightly there.
But the little briar became even sadder.....
And burdened down with care.

It was bad enough living in a ditch.....
But to live among all the blooms,
Surely if the gardener had known,
For me there'd be no room.

But after a few weeks.....
The tiny briar rose...burst aflame,
And now that little thorny briar,
Well, he'll never be the same.

THE LITTLE THORNY BRIAR *Continued...*

The Lord is our gardener…..
And He knows our weak stock,
He knows our evil nature,
That it's as hard as a rock.

But if we surrender our will to the Gardener…..
He'll give us a nature brand new,
And then by His matchless grace…..
He'll make a new person out of you.

1985

FEELINGS

You know so often Christians say, that they want to love others the way God loves them. Well, are those just words, or do they really mean what they're saying? Do they Know what those words actually mean?

If our FEELINGS for others are to be like God's FEELINGS for us, then that means we are to love them unconditionally. And I sometimes think that most people don't really comprehend what unconditional love is. It means that while we were yet sinners, Christ died for us. It means He looked down from the cross and said, "Father, forgive them, for they know not what they do". He forgave the ones who nailed Him to the cross, and yet most people, (even People who say they want to love others unconditionally)want revenge, or at least to have the final say in the matter when anything goes wrong in their lives.

If our FEELINGS are to be like our Father's are for us, then we must be able to love the unlovely exactly the same way we love ourselves. Do we love others enough to put their welfare ahead of our own?

Our feelings are so unstable and our emotions so misleading, that we must never live our lives controlled by either one. When we die to self and let Jesus live and love through us, then that is the one way that we can know that we are loving others as our Father God loves us. He is doing through us what we aren't capable of doing (on our own). So all the glory and the praise belong to Him.

Thank You, Father, that you can put Your feelings in my heart and minister to others through me. You can and will do in and through me, what I could never do myself.

Dear One, surrender your feelings to our Savior and let Him minister through you and you will be truly blessed.

FEELINGS

Your love for me remains the same,
In clear and stormy weather.....
And You promised in Your Word,
That You would never leave me...ever.

Oh, Father, let my feelings,
For other people be.....
Exactly like Your feelings,
Always are for me.

But don't let them be affected,
By what people say or do.....
And let me be impartial,
In all my thoughts and actions too

Help me to love all men the same,
And to see them through Your eyes.....
Until my own eyes close in death,
Or I meet You in the skies.

Others need so much to know You,
Let me be the one to lead their way.....
Not only to salvation,
But to a brighter day.

Only when they find You,
Will they find their way to day from night.....
And may Your Holy Spirit
Give their blinded eyes new sight.

Help me not to live my life,
On feelings or emotions.....
But always on Your Truth,
And not on foolish notions.

For emotions and feelings are misleading
As You would never be.....
So, please, let my thoughts and my emotions,
Be in Your captivity.

1985

161

FEELINGS Continued...

Romans: 12:16 Live in harmony with one another. Do not be proud, but be willing to associate with people of low position. Don't be conceited.

LIFE IS JUST SO BUSY, LORD

How easy it is to let the things of this world crowd out our time with the Lord. And the sad thing about it is, that many times the things that take up our time are good things. The things can even seem to be the very things that the Lord Himself would have us to be doing. But if what we are doing is always leaving us too worn out to take time to pray and read our Bible, then we need to reexamine our priorities.

Many people, especially young couples with children, can easily get over involved in PTA, School projects, sports, ballet, tap, piano lessons and many other good things, and before you know it they find their time with the Lord has become quite rare, and unfortunately the time they do spend with Him is not the quality that it used to be. Often the time they do give to their Father is hurried and insincere.

Suddenly we wonder why we find ourselves all out of sorts. We tend to forget, that when the Lord and His word are our first priority, then everything else seems to fall into its' proper place, and we find ourselves happier and with a lot more peace of mind.

So the next time you feel something is just not right in your life, or in the life of your family, take a look at your priorities and see if they have gotten out of kilter. If so, do whatever you have to, in order to restore the proper balance in your home.

Matthew 6:33 Seek ye first the kingdom of God and His righteousness, and then all these other things shall be added unto you.

LIFE IS JUST SO BUSY, LORD

Do I take time in my busy day,
To pray for those I love?
Or do I in all my busy-ness,
Forget to look above?

I say, "Lord, I'll talk to You later,
When I have more time."
Forgetting that all the things I have…
Are really His not mine.

I think…when I get home,
I really must remember to pray…..
Then I get home and after supper,
Do the dishes…it's been a busy day!

I get in bed and start to pray,
And then, uh oh, I fall asleep…..
I'm so worn out, Lord, You understand,
I'll make a promise I can keep.

I'll pray tomorrow morning, Lord,
I promise that I will…..
Then morning comes and…
Away I go…in a hurry still.

Life is just so busy,
If only I had more time…..
I could say my prayers and read my Bible,
And really, that's not just a line.

Lord, I'm so glad You're not too busy,
To stop and listen when I call…..
I guess it's better calling late,
Than never to call at all.

I can remember in times past,
When life wasn't such a rat race…..
I took time to pray and read Your Word,
Of course…I didn't go at such a fast pace.

Maybe I'll slow down, Lord,
Cause things were better then….
In fact I have to admit,
They were better than they've ever been.

Why did I let the things of this world,
Creep in one by one?
And finally one thing too many crept in,
And I took my eyes off the Son.

But I'm gonna start over and this time,
I'll take time to read and pray…..
Cause I won't forget what it was like,
When I used to say "Tomorrow, Lord."

1985

PRAISE TIME

The privilege of praise is so wonderful and to think we have so much about which to praise the Lord. And the amazing thing about praise is that you can be in the midst of suffering, or be going through some kind of trial, and when you take the time out to stop and praise the Lord, suddenly all your trials and tribulations seem so small and your suffering seems to diminish.

It is so awe inspiring to stop what you're doing and to start singing praise songs or to just start telling God all the things you are thankful for and listing all His fantastic attributes (and the list could go on forever). Just start out by meditating on His character. Father, You are the Alpha and the Omega, the beginning and the end, You are my caregiver, you're the dearest on earth to me, you're my everlasting Father, You're the fairest of ten thousand, You're the God of grace and glory, you're High and lifted up, joy unspeakable, King of all kings, Lord of all Lords, Mercy unending, You're the Name above all names, and we could continue on and on and on………
By meditating on God you begin to realize Who and What He really is to you and to the world.

Praise can turn your gray sky to blue and your night to day. And no matter how bad you may be feeling, you suddenly find yourself feeling a little better. You find that you can praise the hurt away.

We find it so easy to voice all our wants and needs and even the wants and needs of other, and yet we need to spend more time in simple praise.

So many people start off their prayer, Lord, thank You for another day, or thank You for Your many blessings and then they start with their lists of wants and needs or sometimes even gripes and complaints.

Dear One, whether you're driving down the road, you're on your knees, you're taking your bath or sitting in your living room, wherever you are you can praise the Lord. So give it a try today and see if everything doesn't just fall into place. Things go better with praise!

Besides our God is worthy of all of our praise!

Psalm 34:1 His praise will always be on my lips.

Psalm 63:4 I will praise You for as long as I live.

PRAISE TIME

We spend so much time in asking,
For this, that or the other thing.....
We often forget the blessing,
That simply praising His name can bring.

We often start off our prayers with,
"Praise Your name Lord, and thank You for another day"...
but in between the first and last line,
gimme, gimme, gimme seems to be all we can say.

For even when we're asking for others,
We're still asking just the same.....
But you know it might be nice one day,
To just sit and praise His Name.

For when you're sad and lonely,
And you're feeling so low down.....
Start to praise the Lord,
And suddenly things will turn around.

We have the privilege of approaching the throne,
Of the King of Kings and Lord of Lords.....
Of lifting our hands and our hearts in praise,
To the One all heaven adores.

When you stop and think about it,
It's amazing what a little praise time can do.....
It puts our thoughts on the Lord,
And removes that old self from view.

The privilege is always available,
But how often do we take the time.....
To center our prayer on praising the Lord,
Not just listing our needs in each line?

When we cease to praise Him,
Even the very rocks will cry out.....
But, oh, the glory for Him and joy for us,
When we remember what praise is about.

PRAISE TIME Continued...

It's God's Spirit bringing Him glory,
Through the mind and heart of man.....
And love and adoration are put into words,
By His children as best they can.

You can't take the time out to praise Him,
That you're not blessed in body and soul.....
For there's thanksgiving, confession, even intercession,
But without praise a prayer's just not whole.

1985

Psalms 33:1 It is fitting for the upright to praise Him.

TAKE ME IN RETURN

Salvation is a free gift to every believer; available to all men. There is nothing we can do to earn or purchase our salvation. And once we accept Christ as our own personal Lord and Savior there is nothing we can do to pay Him back for what He's done for us. We may feel like we owe Him something but there is no payment due.

But the sensible thing for any child of God to do is to give their life to Jesus, to use in any way that He chooses. Knowing that when we surrender all to the Lord, He will fill us with Himself and do His work through us. But the amazing thing about it is that we are the ones who are so tremendously blessed when we allow the Lord to use us.

Although we are blessed, God is the one Who gets all the glory, for He is actually the one doing the work, we are simply the vessel He has chosen to use.

What a fantastic privilege to be used by the King of Kings and Lord of Lords to accomplish His plan. There is no greater blessing in all of creation than to be used by God.

Thank You, Father, for allowing these vessels made of clay, to be used by Your Son to accomplish Your work.

II Corinthians 4:7 We have this treasure in jars of clay to show that this all surpassing power is from God and not from us.

TAKE ME IN RETURN, LORD

There's a crimson fountain,
Flowing full and free......
Not just for others,
But for a sinner like me.

How can it be,
That a King would come and die.....
For a lost unworthy soul,
For one such as I?

Oh, Precious, Holy One,
Gift from God above.....
Sent to buy my pardon,
With undying love.

A FREE gift.....
Yet, how can it be?
And I only have myself,
To give you back you see

I know I owe nothing,
For salvation comes to me.....
With no strings attached,
It's absolutely free.

But....
Please, take me in return Lord,
For nothing more can I do.....
Than for giving you to me,
I give myself to you.

I know it's not much,
But it's all I have to give.....
In exchange for my salvation
Your life through me to live.

1985

THE BLOOD IS HERE TO STAY

The Blood is Here to Stay is a poem about Pilate not having the backbone to do the right thing, because he was too concerned about what the people would say and do and what the crowd wanted. Apparently Pilate wanted to be a crowd pleaser. Unfortunately many people today are the same way. They want to accept Jesus as their Savior, and they know it would be the right thing to do, but they are so concerned about what their friends might think, that they put off the decision and some never get another opportunity. Had they known that they wouldn't live long enough to get another chance they probably would have made a different decision.

Remember, you too will make a final decision one of these days and I pray that it will be the right one. The choice to be in heaven for eternity or to be in hell is all up to you. There is no riding the fence. It's heaven or hell. Which one will you choose my friend?

Endless hope or a hopeless end?

Don't be a crowd pleaser!

THE BLOOD IS HERE TO STAY

Pilate knew Jesus was a righteous man,
So when the people demanded His life....
Pilate went to the laver and washed his hands,
He didn't want to pay the high price.

He didn't want innocent blood on his hands,
But he didn't want to disappoint the crowd.....
They all wanted Barabbas set free,
And their shouts had become very loud.

First he sent Jesus to Herod,
But he didn't want to make the decision.....
Then Herod sent Jesus back again,
Which put Pilate in a state of derision.

Jesus comes to each person at sometime in their life,
Then each must make a choice.....
To accept Him as Savior, Lord and King,
Or to simply ignore that still, small voice.

When it comes to the blood of Jesus,
There's just no washing it away.....
It's the only means of covering our sin,
There is no other way.

The blood is there to condemn or set free,
The choice is in your control.....
Be washed in the blood and be set free,
Or reject it and lose your soul.

You can freely choose to follow the King,
Or like Pilate...listen to the devil's call.....
The choice is up to you alone,
And it comes to one and all.

You can't send Him away forever,
Without saying yes or no.....
You can try to push Him out of your thoughts,
But it seems He just won't go.

THE BLOOD IS HERE TO STAY Continued...

You'll make a final decision,
But hear me when I say…..
You can wash your hands in the laver,
But the blood is here to stay.

Condemned or set free,
The choice is yours my friend…..
An eternity of ENDLESS HOPE,
Or an eternity with a HOPELESS END.

1985

John 18:39-40 Pilate asked the crowd, "do you want me to release the King of the Jews?" They shouted back, "No not Him! Give us Barabbas!"

I WONDER WHO'S WATCHING

Dear saint of God, have you ever wondered how our friends and loved ones who have gone home to be with the Lord… feel about the things we say and do? Would your behavior change someway if you knew for sure that they were able to see you from heaven?

I know there are things that I have said or done that I am ashamed of and I wish I would have stopped to think before I spoke or acted. I can remember as a child not doing some of the things my friends did because I always thought I don't want to do that because somehow Mother, or MeMe or someone I loved might find out and they would be so disappointed in me, and I didn't want to let them down.

The funny thing is we worry about what other people might think, but do we worry enough about what our Savior thinks? We know that Jesus is with us wherever we go, so, that means if we go places we shouldn't we take Him with us, and if we say things we shouldn't He hears us and whatever we do that we shouldn't He sees us. Do we care? Are we ashamed of ourselves enough to repent and do better? I hope so.

Hebrews 12:1-2 Seeing we are surrounded by such a great cloud of witnesses, let us lay aside every weight and the sin that so easily besets us, and run with patience the race that is set before us looking unto Jesus the author and finisher of our faith.

I WONDER WHO'S WATCHING

If there's a window in heaven,
I wonder who's looking through…..
And if there's anyone's looking,
Well, what about the view?

Would we be sorry when we get there,
To find out how amazed…..
Angels, friends and loved ones were,
When down to earth they gazed.

And if we thought they were looking,
Would our behavior change someway…..
Or would we always put off changing,
For a more convenient day?

Would they be disappointed,
If they could see the things we do?
Well, I hate to tell you brother,
But do I have news for you.

I don't know about our friends and loved ones,
But our Savior, Lord and King…..
We drag Him through the mud so much,
It's become a common thing.

Since Jesus dwells within us,
Whatever we say or do…..
I want you to know, my friend,
We expose Him to it too.

When I think of the places people go,
And some of the things they say…..
It nearly breaks my heart,
We've allowed it to get this way.

Some of the things we wallow in,
Would shock a simple man…..
Just think of how our Savior feels,
When we drag Him through it…by the hand.

I WONDER WHO'S WATCHING Continued...

So let's let Jesus come in,
And clean up our lives…..
Before we find it's too late,
And our last day arrives,

Let Him guide us each day,
In all we say and do …..
And then we won't have to worry about,
What we're dragging Him through.

1985

Galatians 2:20 I am crucified with Christ, and yet I live, yet not I but Christ lives within me.

OUR CHILDREN

Our children are a gift from God and if more people understood that maybe we would take raising them much more seriously. You are told in Proverbs 22:6 to train a child up in the way he should go and in later years he will not depart from it. To me that says, that whatever they are trained to do as a child they will continue to do as adults. Garbage in and garbage out as the old saying goes.

If you constantly criticize, condemn and accuse your children, then you are teaching them not only to do the same thing, but they will become discouraged and it says in scripture in Ephesians 6:4 Fathers do not exasperate your children, in stead bring them up in the training and instruction of the Lord. And in Colossians 3:21 Fathers, do not embitter your children, or they will become discouraged.

Many times I believe people pass on bad child rearing habits from their own childhood. And yet we know the cycle can be broken. When you become a believer in the Lord Jesus Christ, He will give you the perfect parenting skills, if you want Him to and if you ask Him to.

Unfortunately there are those parents who take out their frustrations on their children, and they may not even realize they are doing it. That's why it is so important to be in your Bible and in prayer daily. You also need to be having devotions with your children almost from birth. Make it fun and enjoyable so they will look forward to that time every evening, and not get to where they resent you forcing them to do something they don't want to do.

Never tell your child, "Do as I say and not as I do". Your life should be a godly example for them to follow, and it should lead them to a right relationship with the Lord Jesus Christ, and into becoming godly Christian young men and women.

Raising our children is probably the most critical responsibility we are given as Christians and we need to take it very seriously. Although we may make some mistakes along the way we need to be open and honest with our children and apologize when we are wrong and they will respect us all the more for it. Never be ashamed to admit you're wrong, it's like confessing your sin and it cleans the slate.

Keep a clean slate!

OUR CHILDREN

Oh, Father, why is it,
That our children are grown.......
Before we suddenly realize,
The harm that we've done?

The cruel words we say,
And the scars they can leave....
They cut like a knife,
And make the heart grieve.

We say we love our children,
They're precious gifts from above....
But do our actions fit our words,
And truly show our love?

We hug and we kiss them,
Then criticize and condemn.....
A losing battle for our kids,
And it's one they can't win.

We must get our lives together,
And let the Lord have full, complete control,
Of our thoughts, words and deeds,
Of our body, mind and soul.

So often people say,
"do as I say...not as I do....."
but the words that we say,
they don't always ring true.

In the lives of our children,
We will reap what we sow.....
So the curse...or the blessing,
Is our choice as they grow.

1985

Proverbs 22:6 Train up a child in the way he should go and in later years he will not depart from it.

Ephesians 6:4 Fathers, do not exasperate your children; instead bring them in the training and instruction of the Lord.

TEARS

Dear One, have you ever noticed how beautiful everything is after a rain storm? Although at first some flowers and even some trees can seem a little battered and beaten down by the heavy rain, soon they are upright and more beautiful than ever. And then there are times when it doesn't rain that hard but it's just a light, steady rain; and then immediately everything just seems so new and refreshed.

Well, there are times that the Lord allows circumstances to come into our lives that bring us to tears. They may be tears of joy, sorrow, sadness or repentance but our Father has His purpose in allowing these things to touch our lives. But regardless of the reason for the tears, they seem to have a cleansing effect on our body, soul and spirit. Tears have a way of clearing our thinking and after the crying spell we always feel a little better.

Whatever the reason for our tears, there are many scriptures in our bibles that refer to tears. And after all God Himself gave us the capacity to shed tears for a reason and a purpose.

Personally I have always been a weeper, and I cry if I'm happy, sad or feeling guilty, about something the Holy Spirit has convicted me of doing or thinking or saying. And I know for a fact after a good crying spell I always feel better and I am usually much more sensitive to the voice of the Spirit.

So, dear saint of God, the next time you feel like crying, let her rip! It's the Lord washing the windows of your soul, and that gives you more spiritual insight when your windows are clean!

Psalm 126:5-6 Those who sow in tears will reap in joy. He who goes out weeping, carrying seed to sow, will return with songs of joy, carrying sheaves with him.

Psalm 30:5 weeping may endure for the night but joy cometh in the morning.

John 11:35 Jesus wept.

TEARS

There may come a time in your life,
When blue skies turn to gray…..
When your tears fall like the rain,
All through the lonely night and day.

Remember to trust your heavenly Father,
Until the gray clouds pass away…..
For with the passing of the clouds,
Comes His bright light to show the way.

Trust Him when you think your heart,
Has broken in a million pieces…..
You feel as if your spirit's crushed,
And the pain just never ceases.

For the tears that pour like rain,
Will wash the windows of your soul…..
And it will give God's Holy Spirit,
His full, complete control.

It sometimes takes our tears,
And the pain of a broken heart…..
To purge out all the sin,
And give the Lord a new place to start.

For joy is not the absence of suffering,
But the presence of the Lord above…..
Putting broken pieces back in place,
By His matchless power and love.

Our Father is never closer to His children,
Than when their broken hearts are in His hands…..
And the tears that poured like rain,
Are dried by the One who cares and understands.

For He mends their broken hearts,
And suddenly the dark clouds roll away…..
With their tears…He wipes the windows of their souls,
So they can see…it's a bright, new day!

1985

TEARS Continued...

Psalms 126:5 Those who sow in tears will reap with songs of joy.

Rev.21:4 And He shall wipe away every tear from their eyes.

THE THIEF

When you think about the crucifixion of Jesus, usually all we think about is Jesus and the suffering that He went though for us. But there were two other people crucified with Jesus that day. One criminal was on His right and one was on His left. Both criminals were guilty of their crimes but they reacted in two different ways.

I believe those criminals represent us and we are all guilty before God, but each person handles their guilt in a different way. Some people try to lie and say they're not guilty, while others admit their guilt and yet try to bargain their way out of trouble. Others admit they are guilty and grieve over their sin and willingly accept their punishment. We all know we deserve to be punished for our sin and that we deserve to go to hell. But some choose to accept the payment Jesus made for us on the cross, and others think that there is something they themselves can do to pay for their sin and they won't believe that Jesus' payment was enough. Foolishly people refuse to accept the free gift of salvation and try to pay for their sins their own way, and yet there is no other way.

Some people when confronted with their guilt, rant and rave like the thief on one side of Jesus. They don't think their punishment is fair, or pretend they're not guilty. But we are all guilty before God and there is only one acceptable payment for our sin and that is the blood of Jesus, and His blood covers every sin. We only have to accept His payment in order to live in heaven for Eternity. Don't be like the thief that ranted and raved and mocked Jesus, but be like the other thief that acknowledged his sin, and asked Jesus not to forget him. Because of his faith he was in paradise with Jesus before the day was over.

Thank you Father, that You loved us so much that You sent Your Son to die for us. Thank You Jesus, that You loved us enough to die for us. Help us, Father, to love You enough to live for You, and to let You live in and through us.

Help us to see ourselves as You see us and to admit and confess any sin that we commit. We don't want any barriers between us. I John 1:9 Psalm 66:18

THE THIEF

The thief hung there on the cross, suspended in space,
Knowing he was there for a reason, and that he could not deny.....
But the man in the middle, he had committed no crime,
Yet He was nailed to a cross, and The Thief wondered, why?

He heard one man say, "Father, forgive them",
the other one was ranting and raving.....
Why would a man in such pain, say Father, forgive?
The Thief didn't know... that the world needed saving.

He knew he deserved to suffer for his crime,
But what about the man in the middle.....
He didn't deserve this, so why did He have to die?
This must be some strange kind of riddle.

The one criminal mocked Jesus as he hung on the cross,
The other said, "We deserve the punishment we've been given."
"But this man is innocent of any crime, and yet....
The crowd seems strangely driven."

The Thief said, "Jesus remember me...when You come into Your
kingdom."
He didn't know Jesus was dying...so that He could save the lost.
Jesus told him, "today you'll be with me in paradise,"
But the thief had no idea of how much paradise cost.

The two thieves on the crosses beside Jesus,
Represent you and me and the choices we make......
Jesus suffered unjustly for those who justly should suffer,
Just how much should one man have to take?

Yet without Jesus' unjust suffering...The whole world would be bound for
hell.....
But by His grace and His death on the cross,
Those who before were lost and hopeless,
Are now no longer hopelessly lost

Not only would The Thief be in paradise that day,
But the gates of heaven had been opened for all mankind.....
The price for man's sin at last had been paid,
Now no one need be left behind.

THE THIEF Continued...

So my friend, will you be ranting and raving over your situation,
Even though the situation is of your own making?
Or will you repent and put your trust in Jesus,
And like The Thief...find heaven can be yours for the taking?

Luke 23:339-43 One of the criminals who hung there hurled insults at Him: "Aren't you the Christ? Save yourself and us!" But the other rebuked him. "Don't you fear God," he said, "since you are under the same sentence? We are punished justly, for we are getting what our deeds deserve. But this man has done nothing wrong." Then he said, "Jesus, remember me when you come into your kingdom." Jesus answered him, "I tell you the truth, today you will be with me in paradise."

ALL IS NOT RIGHT

Have you ever been to a church where certain people were frowned upon and in fact there were certain classes of people who would not be welcome in the church. Well, I have seen pastors that acted like they wanted a rich, well-dressed congregation only. You just have to wonder where those people are going to be the day that Jesus calls His children home. Will they be left standing in the pulpits and sitting in the pews, if the Rapture takes place on Sunday?

Is that kind of behavior pleasing to the Lord? I don't think so! The scriptures talk about being humble, having a broken and contrite heart, about loving the unlovely.

Some people in church spend more time looking around to see what people are wearing than they do listening to the word. We need to be more concerned about our spiritual growth than somebody else's station in life. What did Jesus do and where did Jesus go. Who did Jesus hang around with besides the disciples? Who did Jesus and the disciples reach out to? Should we do any less?

Help us Father to see each person through Your eyes and to see and meet their needs by Your strength and grace. Help us to allow You to love the unlovely through us and to be grateful that You would give us the privilege of loving and serving others who may be less fortunate than we are.

John 4:20 If anyone says, "I love God," yet hates his brother, he is a liar. For anyone who does not love his brother, whom he has seen, cannot love God, whom he has not seen.

ALL IS NOT RIGHT

The sky is blue,
And the sun shines bright.....
Yet in this world,
Something's not right.

A soft gentle breeze,
Carries puffs of white clouds.....
But there's death in the air,
And it's falling on the crowds.

Walking in the forest,
You can hear the babbling brook.....
Yet, walking down the street,
Faces have a forlorn look.

Preachers in the churches...preaching the Word,
And the choirs are singing their hymns.....
And then there's the congregation,
Standing in their sins.

Looking oh, so pious,
Right down their nose.....
At the poor fellow who just walked in,
In his worn-out clothes.

Where's the care and concern,
About that lost soul.....
There are walking dead about us,
And they're in Satan's control.

Where's the unselfish love for our brother,
Who might have lost his way.....
The care for the walking wounded,
Who needs help...not tomorrow...but today.

We're spiritually alive,
And yet we act like we're dead.....
We're children of the King,
But we walk around like paupers instead.

We dread having to take the time,
To reach out and offer a hand…..
Someone might take us up on it,
And then where would we stand?

Lord, break us and make us,
Into vessels You can use…..
And never allow us,
Your gifts to misuse.

In fact, Father, break our hearts,
And give us contrite spirits…..
And bring us to the place
Where we can see the lost and dying near us.

1985

James 2:5-6 Has not God chosen those who are poor in the eyes of the world to be rich in faith? And to inherit the kingdom He promised those who love Him. But you have insulted the poor.

PRAY

I've heard that even an atheist prays in a foxhole. And Saint of God, sadly that is practically true of some Christians. When things go wrong or we have a need or an emergency the first thing we do is turn to God. Well, how would you feel if your family or friends only talked to you when they wanted something? If you never had any simple everyday conversations, would you feel like they really cared anything about you? Wouldn't you feel like you were just being used?

I wonder how God feels when the only time we talk to Him is when we have a need? Wouldn't it be the right thing to do, if we talked to our Father about everything? When we don't have a need and we take the time to talk to Him about how great He is and how much we appreciate Him, and we praise His name just because He is worthy of our praise.

It's so easy to talk to God, because we can do it in our closet on our knees, or driving down the road, or when we're in bed, or sitting at the table or even in the bathtub. We have absolutely no excuse for not having long, frequent conversations with our Heavenly Father.

Dear brothers and sisters in Christ, let's make the conscious decision to put forth every effort to talk to our Father on a much more regular basis and to change the tempo and content of our new prayer life. Let's vow to praise and adore Him more and to let Him know how much we appreciate Him. Let's be sure to pray for others more and ourselves less, for our Father already knows our needs before we voice them.

Prayer is so far reaching, it goes from us on earth to our Father in heaven and can have a life changing effect right in our own life, our own home or clear across the world. It's just awesome, and such a privilege. Why don't more people take advantage of it?

Father, help us to realize what You have done for us by giving us the wonderful privilege of prayer and let Your Holy Spirit remind us to take full advantage of that blessing.

I Thessalonians 5:16-19 Rejoice always, PRAY without ceasing, in everything give thanks, for this is the will of God in Christ Jesus concerning you. Quench not the Spirit, despise not prophecies, hold fast to that which is good and abstain from all appearance of evil.

PRAY

Pray… when life goes on,
Like a mighty river calmly flows…..
Like a walk in forest green,
With birds singing soft and low.

Pray when there is no pain,
And when there is no sorrow…..
When at the end of the day,
You can look forward to tomorrow.

Pray when day skies are blue,
And night's stars are clearly seen…..
When we feel so at peace,
And life seems so serene.

Pray, when darkness looms on the horizon,
And storm clouds come rolling in…..
When the battle starts to rage,
And you're running low on friends.

Pray and remember,
GOD STILL REIGNS…from His mighty throne on high…..
And His arm is never too short,
To reach us from the sky.

Prayer can pierce through the deepest gloom,
And bring down light from heaven above…..
It can wind its' way to glory,
And come back with God's own love.

Pray in Jesus name my friend,
For He has all the battles won…..
And God answers every prayer,
When it's offered in the name of His SON.

1985

I Thess.5:16 Be joyful always; pray continually; give thanks in all circumstances, for this is God's will for you in Christ Jesus.

LORD SHOW MY FRIEND THE WAY

Dear One, have you ever had a friend that you loved dearly, but they didn't know Jesus as their Savior and you wanted the peace of knowing that they were going to be in heaven someday?

I have had friends that were such wonderful worldly people and yet they acted totally unconcerned about the future. They never seemed to worry about the fact that if they died they were going straight to hell, but I worried about it.

In many cases we even have family members who don't know Jesus and we desperately want them to come to that saving knowledge of the Savior. Well, friend we must be willing to pray whatever it takes Father, then please, bring it into their life in order to get them to see their lost condition and their need for Christ as Savior. It may be painful circumstances that they will have to go through, but when you love someone you want them to be in heaven someday and the pain will be worth it in the end.

Pray without ceasing for that lost soul and never give up until they take their last breath. They'll thank you for all eternity that you bugged them until they gave up and gave in to Jesus.

Thank You Father, for the privilege of sharing the Gospel with a lost and dying world.

LORD, SHOW MY FRIEND THE WAY

Lord, give my friend a hunger,
That nothing else will satisfy…..
A hunger for Your Word and love and peace,
Things that money can never buy.

A desire to know Your Word,
In a real and personal way…..
To know they're bound for glory,
When the trumpet sounds that day.

Fill their heart with such a void,
That nothing else can fill the space…..
None other than the Savior's love,
And Your amazing grace.

For Father, I want my friend,
To know the boundless mercy and love…..
Brought down to earth by Jesus,
From His heavenly throne above.

Let them have a need,
That they think no one can meet…..
A need so great that when it's met,
They'll fall down at Your feet.

For if my friend never has a problem,
They'll never experience Your power…..
And if everything's always grand,
Will they look forward to that hour?

The hour when You'll come to call,
Whether in death or Rapture sweet…..
The hour when You'll take us home,
To gather at Your Mercy Seat.

You see Lord, I love my friend a lot,
And I'm concerned about their soul…...
And I want them to be there,
When You call that final roll.

So, if it takes some hard times,
And even some tears now and then…..
Bring them on Lord, and if You have to,
Then bring them on again.

I want my friend to know You,
And to be in heaven some day…..
And dear Lord, only You,
Can show my friend the way.

1985

MAKING MEMORIES

While we are living in this world we are making lasting memories. We are forming an impression of ourselves that we will leave behind when we go home to be with the Lord. Our actions and our words will make an impression on the person or persons that see the actions or hear the words. Are we making a godly impression or an ungodly one?

If Jesus is living in us, then don't you think, when people see us or talk to us, that when we leave their presence we should leave a pleasant, lingering feeling of contentment and joy?

What would you want to see in your obituary in the newspaper, or written on your headstone at the cemetery? Wouldn't it be a blessing if your family put SHE LOVED THE LORD or HE WALKED WITH GOD? If we could look down from heaven and see our loved ones after we're gone, wouldn't we want them to be thankful that we were in their lives? We wouldn't want them to be saying or thinking, I loved him/her but in some ways I'm glad he/she's gone. Saying "I know he/she meant well but".....

Live a life that's pleasing to the Lord, and I'm sure it will be pleasing to your family, and to all those who know you as well.

Hebrews 12:1-2 Therefore, since we are surrounded by such a great cloud of witnesses, let us throw off everything that hinders and the sin that so easily besets us, and let us run with patience the race that is set before us, looking unto Jesus, the author and finisher of our faith.

Be a blessing, dear one!

MAKING MEMORIES

When I've left this world below,
And gone to heaven above......
Will the thoughts I leave behind,
Reflect His goodness and His love?

When my loved ones sit and dream,
Of times and days gone by.....
Will they rejoice in their memories,
Or will they just sit and cry?

Will their memories bring them grief,
Over time wasted and unused?
I pray of these two things,
That I will never be accused.

Father, help me to use the time,
That You've allotted me.....
Being a channel of Your love,
To friends and family.

May I ever tell the story,
Of salvation to the lost.....
Of the cruel cross of Calvary,
And just how much it cost.

May I use each day and hour,
Bringing love and joy to those nearby.....
Until the day I leave this world,
And meet You in the sky.

When friends and loved ones pause to think about,
The memories I've left behind.....
May just the very thought of me,
Bring only You to mind.

For I have no desire to be remembered,
For any other thing.....
Than that I walked with God,
And made some sad hearts sing.

1985

194

MAKING MEMORIES Continued...

I Peter 2:12 Live such good lives among the pagans that, though they accuse you of doing wrong, they may see your good works and glorify God on the day He visits us.

I'LL TAKE AND I'LL GIVE

Dear One, have you ever noticed that the Lord Jesus not only gave His life so that we could live, but He takes our pain and sorrow and our poverty and loss, and since we've been saved we can never be lost.

Our wonderful Savior takes all our negatives and turns them into positives. He says, "take my yoke upon you, for my yoke is easy and my burden is light." He says, "Cast your burden on me and I will sustain you". Jesus said, "By my stripes you are healed".

Jesus does everything for us and asks nothing in return, except that we receive His free gift of salvation. Jesus is the ultimate giver, the ultimate servant. I can't really think of anything that Jesus ever did just for Himself. He was born, lived and died for us. Such love we cannot comprehend, but oh, my friend, thank God for it! And if only we would be like him!

Father, please help us to be like Jesus, help us to be servants! Servants of the king and happy and joyful in our position.

I'LL TAKE AND I'LL GIVE

Jesus says, "I love you,
And I'll gladly take your pain…..
I'll suffer your loss,
And give you my gain.

My child, because I love you,
I'll suffer your sorrow…..
And when you have a need,
There'll be no need to borrow.

I'll take your poverty,
And give you my wealth…..
I'll suffer your sickness,
And give you good health.

I'll take your grief,
And I'll give you my joy…..
So, from now on, that old sorrow,
you'll never employ.

I gave you life,
And yet you gave me death.
Still, I'll always be with you,
Until you take your last breath.

I'll bear the storms,
The wind and the rain….
I'll give you blue skies and sunshine,
When you call on my name.

Dear One, I'll meet your needs,
No matter the cost…..
And now that you're found,
You can never be lost.

For I'll never leave you,
But I'll give and I'll take….
And everything I've done,.
I've done for your sake."

2005

197

Matthew 20:28 Just as the Son of Man did not come to be served, but to serve, and to give His life as a ransom for many.

Isaiah 53:4-5 Surely He took up our infirmities and carried our sorrows, yet we considered Him stricken by God, smitten by Him, and afflicted. But He was pierced for our transgressions, He was crushed for our iniquities; the punishment that brought us peace was upon Him, and by His wounds we are healed.

A FIT VESSEL

It is so easy to say, "I want the Lord to use me", but the question is how much? Do we want to be a fit vessel for His use? If so we must be willing to allow Him to make us into vessels fit for His service.

Sometimes we have to ask God, to reveal any hidden or secret faults we may have, in fact, we may not even realize that we have any, but if we're willing He can reveal those to us through His Holy Spirit.

Are we willing to ask ourselves, "How do I look to God?", and when we ask Him to show us how we look to Him, when he does, we have to be willing to face the facts and do something about it. Sometimes we find ourselves, going through some pretty hard times, that the Lord has to allow us to go through in order for us to become what He wants us to be.

Once we can be used by God, it is so important for us to constantly examine ourselves and to keep any known sins confessed, for we know that He doesn't even hear our prayers when we have any unconfessed sin in our lives.Ps.66:18

At times the chastening rod can be pretty painful, but afterward it yields the peaceable fruit of righteousness unto those who are exercised by it. Heb.12:11

The Lord disciplines those He loves and scourges every son whom He receives. Heb.12:6

Let the Lord make you into a fit vessel for His use and you will eventually find greater joy than you have ever known. For nothing this world has to offer can compare to being used by the King of Kings and the Lord of Lords.

A FIT VESSEL

Lord, let all the desires of my heart…be acceptable in your sight,
And all my earthly works be done, not by mine…but…by Your might.

May I never allow…evil desires, to have any place in my thoughts.
Help me remember the wages of sin, and just how much they cost.

Not just the sins of the world…but my own sin and strife,
They cause me… suffering and shame…but they cost Jesus…
His precious life.

May the words that I speak be pleasing… not just to others… but to You,
And every sound I utter…be always trustworthy and true.

Set a watch at my mouth….and keep the door to my lips.
They both are in Your hands…to use for Your honor and glory,
And to fulfill Your righteous demands.

Since a vessel fit…for Your use…I desire to be,
Please, let Your Holy Spirit…reveal my sin to me.

For one evil thought left unconfessed, can soon be two…not one,
And then instead of just a thought, an evil deed is done.

So, search me Father and show me…just what lies within…..
For in my heart and mind, I don't want to harbor sin.

Cleanse me from those secret faults…that You may find in me...
That on my own…I'm unable …to look inside and see.

Then let the words from my lips…praise Your precious Holy Name…
My thoughts and my deeds…may they do the very same.

1989

Psalms 139:23-24 Search me oh, God, and know my heart, try me and know my anxious thoughts. See if there be any wicked way in me, and lead me in the way everlasting.

Psalms 19:12-14 Who can understand his errors, keep back thy servant from willful sins and let them not have dominion over me. may the words of my mouth and the meditations of my heart be acceptable in thy sight, Oh, Lord my strength and my Redeemer.

THE REAL MEANING OF CHRISTMAS

What is the real meaning of Christmas? That God Himself took on flesh and became a baby in a manger, so that He could live 33 years and die a cruel death on a cross. all because of love. We cannot fathom such love, for would we be willing to suffer and die for those who spit on us and beat us and abused us? Or would we send our precious son to suffer so horribly for the very ones who crucified Him?

We get so caught up in the parties and the shopping and the gift giving that we tend to forget, WHERE WOULD WE BE WITHOUT CHRISTMAS, and yet the world is trying to take Christ out of Christmas. Not only out of Christmas, but out of everything. Off the money, out of the schools, out of our conversation (employees can't even wish customers merry Christmas. Now it's Happy Holidays) and yet, there would be no reason for the holiday without Jesus.

Thank You Jesus, for being born for us, for dying for us, and for living in us. May Your birthday become the most awesome celebration of all times, but for all the right reasons, not just a time to spend money on unneeded presents. If we buy someone a gift let it be in Your memory. Let all the gifts given at Christmas, be given for Your birthday and for Your glory. Given to someone to bring them joy in Your name. Let the gifts come from You through the giver and go to the You in the receiver. If the receiver is not a believer in Jesus, may they become one through the love shown by the giver.

Forgive us for forgetting You at Christmas and help us to do better next year. In fact, help us to celebrate Your birthday everyday, not just one day out of the year.

THE REAL MEANING OF CHRISTMAS

Christmas is a special time,
For friends and loved ones dear.....
For many folks...it seems to be,
Their favorite time of year.

It's that time for parties,
And shopping at the mall.....
Everyone seems so happy,
They're spreading cheer to one and all.

It's time for wrapping presents,
They'll be opened with delight,,,,,
Are you getting what you want?
You never know you just might.

But the real meaning of Christmas,
The birth of God's dear Son.....
Usually seems forgotten,
We're having so much fun.

Christmas isn't the presents,
But I guess you could say it's the tree.....
After all Jesus was born to die,
On a tree at Calvary.

Christmas is the time,
We should celebrate His birth.....
God Himself took on flesh,
And came to dwell on earth.

And no greater gift was ever given,
Than when God gave us His Son.....
So this year let's not forget it,
Because we're having too much fun.

This year let the gifts we give,
Be a special revelation.....
To the giver and the receiver,
Of God's so great salvation.

THE REAL MEANING OF CHRISTMAS
Continued...

It's truly a time for celebration,
But let's not forget the reason…..
For without the birth of Jesus,
There'd be no reason for the season.

So don't mess with the message of Christmas,
It's been the same for over 2000 years…..
Jesus came and died to pay for our sins,
Now that gives us a reason to cheer.

2005

Happy Birthday, Jesus!

Luke 1:31 You will be with child and give birth to a son, and you are to call His name, Jesus.

I Peter 3:15 Be ready always to give an answer to every man that asks a reason for the hope that is in You, with meekness and fear.

LOSS IS SOMETIMES GAIN

Saint of God, there are times when our loving, heavenly Father has to remove someone or something from our lives, and it is always for our good. Although at the time that loss may seem far greater than we can bear, there is always a good reason for our Father to take this measure. We must truly believe with all our hearts, that He loves us and He would never do or allow anything in our lives that was not for our good.

I found in my own life that whatever God has taken away He has replaced with something better. Even though at the time of the loss I might have been saddened or disappointed, I always knew in my heart that my Father only wanted what was best for me. It's the same way with our own children, when we have to take something away from them, it's always for a good reason and at times we even replace that thing with something better for them.

If we trust our heavenly Father, and have a blind faith in Him, we will always know He is doing what is best for us. He gave us many examples in scripture of Old and New Testament saints that had to give up a lot, and all they could do was trust Him. When you start to be discouraged about some loss, consider Job, Jacob, Joseph, Paul, all the Disciples and many others.

Remember Dear One, your Father loves you and only wants what is best for you. Weeping endures for the night but joy comes in the morning. And truly, LOSS IS SOMETIMES GAIN for the child of God.

As the old hymn says, "Trust Him and never doubt and He will surely bring you out". And always remember that a blessing is waiting just on the other side of the circumstance.

Job 1:20-22 At this, Job got up and tore his robe and shaved his head. Then he fell to the ground in worship and said: "Naked I came from my mother's womb, and naked I will depart. The Lord gave and the Lord has taken away; may the name of the Lord by praised."

LOSS IS SOMETIMES GAIN

There are things in this world,
We think we can't live without.....
Then the Lord, in His wisdom,
Let's us find out.

He causes us to realize,
That LOSS IS SOMETIMES GAIN.....
And sometimes what He takes away,
He gives us back again.

The Lord gave Isaac back his son,
And then He gave Jacob back his son.....
And everything the devil stole,
He gave Job back and then some!

When we become a child of God,
We give our lives to Him...
To add to...or...take away from,
The things that lead to sin.

For some reason... people think of sin,
As murder, stealing or lying.....
And yet we find in God's word,
That so is denying.

Denying we are wrong,
When we're really not right.....
If we foolishly continue,
It will dim our spiritual sight.

Sometimes we unfortunately think,
We've almost spiritually "arrived".....
But then the Lord shows us,
That fact..........is denied.

Often He must take away,
A thing that seems most dear....
And it almost breaks our hearts,
But still... we know our God is near.

We know our Father has a reason,
When we suffer loss…..
And although it hurts us to suffer,
He suffered… so much greater …on the cross.

For when God takes away,
Anything from our lives…..
It's for a higher purpose,
That you can definitely surmise.

Whatever Jesus takes away,
He replaces it with something better…..
And His provisions always meet,
Our need right to the letter.

1989

Philippians 4:19 And my God shall supply all your needs according to His riches in glory by Christ Jesus.

THE RACE

The poem THE RACE came to me after reading the Scripture in Hebrews 12:1-3Since we are surrounded by such a great cloud of witnesses, let us throw off everything that hinders and the sin that so easily entangles us. And let us run with perseverance the race that is set before us. Let us fix our eyes on Jesus, the author and finisher of our faith, Who for the joy that was set before Him endured the cross, scorning its' shame, and sat down at the right hand of the throne of God.

It's as if we are all running a race on a track surrounded by the crowd in the grandstands. The angels and all the saints who have gone before are watching, and cheering us on. Can't you just hear them when the devil is tempting us and we don't give in? And then there are those times that we do stumble and fall (give in to temptation). The crowd in the grandstands probably goes oh, no! And then when they see us get up and keep running, they are back cheering for us.

Just as Paul told Timothy in II Timothy 4:7-8 I have fought a good fight, I have finished my course, I have kept the faith. Now there is laid up for me a crown of Righteousness, which the Lord, the righteous Judge will give unto me, but not unto me only, but unto all them also, who love His appearing.

Whenever we fall, it is so important for us to get back up, brush ourselves off, and finish our race. We must always remember to REBOUND AND KEEP MOVING. When we sin, we rebound by confessing our sins (I John 1:9) No matter how big or small we think the sin might be, the same procedure must be followed in order to get back in fellowship. It's always best to confess our sins the minute we realize we have Committed them, for until we do, we will remain out of fellowship, and The Lord won't hear our prayers again until we are back in fellowship (I John 1:9) If we confess our sins He is faithful and just to forgive us of our sins and to cleanse us from all unrighteousness.

Run with all your might, and all your strength and Jesus will see you at the finish line.

THE RACE

The angels up in heaven,
And the saints who've gone before.....
Are watching from the grandstands,
To see our final score.

Will they hear the Master say.....
When the race is finally run,
"you have finished your course, my child.....
well done...well done!"

Or will they see us falter.....
And sometimes lag behind?
And then they'll hear us stammer,
When an excuse we cannot find.

Will we persevere until the last,
And do the very best we can?
We may not finish first.....
But we can say we ran!

The Lord knows each runner,
Each in a personal way.....
So, He's the One who'll do the judging,
On that final JUDGMENT DAY.

The ones who find it easy,
To come in at first place,,,,,
May not find as many rewards,
As those who barely finish the race.

It's how you run your race that counts.....
Not the place or show,
Some may run very swiftly,
Others just go along with the flow.

Some who have to labor and toil,
Just to crawl across the line.....
May to their surprise,
Find their own gold mine.

THE RACE Continued...

So let us lay aside the weights.....
And the sins that trip us up,
Don't lose heart...run our best,
And Jesus will give us the winner's cup.

June 25, 1985

II Timothy 4:7-8 I have fought a good fight, I have finished my course, I have kept the faith, henceforth there is laid up for me a crown of righteousness which the Lord, the Righteous judge, will give me but not me only, but also all those who love His appearing.

THIS IS NOT YOUR DAY

This Is Not Your Day is a poem, the Lord gave me for a young man in our church. Vincent and his wife Robin, were a precious young couple, who had been going through some very difficult circumstances and I had been lifting them up in prayer when I felt this burden to write this little poem.

Vincent had some very severe health problems and had been near death on several occasions, but as all Christians know, we are not going home to be with the Lord until He is ready for us. When the time of our homegoing arrives then the Lord will give us His dying grace.

I know the thought of dying can be very frightening, but it is actually the fear of the unknown that is so upsetting to many believers. We must remember how much God loves us and remember that perfect love casts out fear. I can remember as a child that my Daddy wanted me to jump off the side of the pool into his arms and I didn't know how to swim yet. It was a scary thing for a child to jump off into the unknown, but I had faith that my daddy would catch me and that he wouldn't let anything happen to me. Fear of the unknown is a fearfulness that can only be overcome by a complete faith and trust. The death of a believer is much the same way, we are leaping off into something we have never experienced before and it's only natural for there to be some apprehension about the experience, but then you'll find joy unspeakable and indescribable waiting on the other side.

I have to admit, that at times, when I consider the time that the Lord will call me home, I become apprehensive myself, because I don't know the means He will use. It's nothing to be ashamed of. It doesn't mean we don't trust the Lord, I think it is just our bodies reacting to stress and pressure. It's probably a chemical reaction, but God I'm sure understands, after all He made us, and all the chemicals from which we are made. We probably go into preservation mode, and our humanity doesn't understand what the spiritual man understands.

I only know that my God will supply ALL MY NEEDS according to His riches in glory, by Christ Jesus. I know that He will give me the grace to go through certain circumstances, only when the need arises.

If I know He loves me and will supply all my needs as they arise, then I can have overriding peace when the time comes for me to go home. It will be what's best for Carolyn. For our Father definitely wants what is best for all His children, just as we do for ours.

THIS IS NOT YOUR DAY

Dear child of mine,
This is just... not your day.....
You can't come home,
No matter what the doctors say.

I decided the day of your departure,
Before time began.....
So, you can't come home,
Until I tell you, you can.

It doesn't really matter,
What some doctors and test might say.....
For I'm the One who appointed you,
Your homecoming day.

I love you more,
Than you'll ever know....
Even though in the midst of suffering,
It may not seem so.

But precious one, just trust me,
When the days of trouble come.....
And remember I loved you so much,
That I sent my only Son.....

So, let Him be the bearer,
Of all your sorrow and your pain.....
He'll take your burdens upon Himself,
If you'll just call upon His name.

He can set you free,
From all worry, fear and doubt.....
Pretty soon instead of sighing,
You'll be ready to shout!

Well, I may call tomorrow,
Or maybe in 20 years...
But either way, when I call
You'll have no need for fears.

For when you arrive in heaven,
And at last you step on shore…..
You'll say, "Gee Father God,,
This was sure worth waiting for.

2005

John 4:18 There is no fear in love. Perfect love casts out fear. If we are afraid of the future or eternity, we can remind ourselves of God's love. We can resolve our fears by first, focusing on His immeasurable love for us, and then by allowing Him to love others through us. His love will quiet your fears and give you confidence.

TOTAL SURRENDER

Sometimes it's so hard for a believer to understand what TOTAL SURRENDER means. The world is so outspoken on everybody doing their own thing. They feel like what they do is nobody else's business. And many times even a Christian can be caught up in that or a similar frame of mind.

The baby believer has no way of knowing the real joy and happiness that totally surrendering your life to Christ can bring. But a more mature Christian has experienced the Christ directed life, where Christ is on the throne and there is peace, joy and happiness in their life that can only be achieved with a Christ directed life.

All Christians need to let Jesus be in the driver's seat, and they need to take a backseat and allow Jesus to do the driving. Then they will always find their way and wherever they are going they will always get there on time, and in one piece.

So friend, get out of the driver's seat today and TOTALLY SURRENDER the driving to Jesus and enjoy the ride for a change.

You'll never be the same.

TOTAL SURRENDER

Jesus Your Son is Life.
Your precious Holy Word is the strength of Life.
Without either one there would be no Life.

So, Father, where would I be without You?
There would be no reason to live…..
You gave me Your everything,
No less …then I should I give.

I want to give You my all…..
To do with as You will,
I know, You know what's best for me,
Yet, do I hold back still?

Help me, Father, to completely submit,
And to allow You full control…..
Not just giving You part of my life,
But giving You the whole.

Total surrender sounds strange to the world,
So used to "doing its' own thing".
If they only knew the joy and peace…..
The contentment…that surrender can bring.

For when one surrenders their all…..
It not only includes their life,
But it also includes their worthlessness…..
And That ugly, old sin and strife.

When we yield our all to the Master…..
To do with as He will,
He'll guide and direct and carry our load,
In all the world there's no greater thrill.

To think the One Who created everything,
Included me in His plan…..
And if I merely submit to Him,
He'll take and guide me by the hand.

TOTAL SURRENDER *Continued...*

As a Father who loves His children......
He wants only what's best for each one,
But many will never know what they missed,
When they rejected God's only Son.....Life!

1987

THE CAPTAIN OF OUR SHIP

If you were to compare our lives to a tiny little ship, and we are set out on the sea of life, can't you just imagine the fear that would over take us in the midst of any terrible storm that might come up, or even being bumped by a giant whale and nearly capsizing?

The funny thing is that we are somewhat in control of the seas and the storms. Aren't our seas going to be a lot calmer and our sailing a lot smoother when we have our priorities straight and when Jesus has His proper place in our lives? But when we try to be, not only the ship, but the captain as well, things just don't seem to go right. We run into too many rough seas and have too many strange occurrences in the weather.

There are times when we will be able to enjoy calm waters and beautiful cloudless skies and smooth sailing, but things can change in an instant and then even in the midst of the fiercest storm, if we keep our eyes on our captain and place our faith in Him and in His ability to steer our ship, then we will make it safely through.. We may encounter many storms during our lifetime and yet we can have peace in the midst of each storm, it we always give the captain the full control of our ship and let Him steer us safely to our harbor.

Smooth sailing, dear One!

THE CAPTAIN OF OUR SHIP

Our life is like a tiny ship,
Set sail on the sea of life…..
The tempest and the storms,
Are all our heartaches, sin and strife.

The Captain of our ship,
Is the precious Lord above…..
And He keeps our vessel steady,
By His power and by His love.

The winds may violently rage,
And the billows wildly roll…..
But our ever faithful Captain,
He'll never lose control.

When skies grow dark and threatening,
And lightning flashes across the sky…..
…and the once calm and placid waters,
are rolling up ever so high.

We must trust our Captain,
To see our little ship through the storm…..
For He is ever able,
To keep her safe from harm.

And even though the tiny vessel,
May get tossed and blown…..
She'll be sure to reach her port,
When she finally heads for home.

Then when we're nearing harbor,
And our voyage will be no more…..
We can see the angels, our friends and loved ones,
Waiting to welcome us on shore.

1985

Psalms 37:4-5 Delight yourself in the Lord, and He will give you the desires of your heart. Commit your way unto the Lord, trust in Him also and He will bring it to pass.

STORMS

Dear Friend, there are times in our lives that everything just seems to be going right for a change and we're so happy, and suddenly the bottom drops out and everything that can go wrong does.

I believe we just tend to forget, that Jesus is with us through the good times and the bad, and we can actually feel a closeness in the hard times, that we can't feel during the good times. I have felt God's presence in hours of darkness, that is impossible to describe. It is such a precious feeling, that cannot be explained. Unless you have experienced it you won't know what I mean. But when my son was in a critical situation in the hospital, and the doctors really didn't know if he would make it, (even though it's no fun to go through those experiences) I wouldn't trade the time I went through for anything, for I literally felt God's presence carrying me through.

On the other side of the circumstance we can always look back on it and see God working in our lives in some special way. It becomes a sacred thing between us and God.

Even though these trials are hard to go through, they can end up being so precious, that we almost miss them when they are over.

There would be no mountaintops if there were no valleys and how boring life would be if it were all just flat plains. So we should thank God for the mountains but also for the valleys, for when He is with us in the valley it can be just as beautiful or more so than the mountaintop.

The poem STORMS came to me after nearly losing my son when he was 16 years old. God taught me that the storm itself can be beautiful but after the storm we seem to have a peace and rest that surpasses all understanding and it's like everything is new and life is starting all over again.

God Bless you as you walk with the Lord through the mountains and the valleys.

STORMS

The sky is gray and stormy....
The clouds are hanging low....
The rain is pouring down....
And the howling winds blow.

The trees are bending toward earth....
Beaten and battered by the wind.....
How can such a fierce storm....
Seem so much like a long-lost friend?

The little fragile flowers....
Crushed and broken by the rain.....
It seems...with broken stems and petals...
They'll never be the same.

The wind, the rain and the brokenness....
Are all tools in the hands of Him....
Who is the Creator and the Sustainer....
....the Savior of all men.

Although at times they can be fierce and frightening...
And they can cause quite an alarm.....
Yet an unexplainable comfort ....
Can be found in the midst of a storm.

For the awesome power of our God.....
In a storm can be clearly seen.....
And when the storm is over....
It seems almost like a dream.

And then as the earth awakens....
A radiant new beauty can be found....
In what seemed crushed and broken.....
A vibrant new life will abound.

Just remember......

We are never closer to the power of the Lord....
Than in the midst of the storms and strife.....
And after the storm will come a healing....
A brand new day...a whole new lease on life.

1985

STORMS Continued...

II Cor.4:7-9 We have this treasure in earthen vessels to show that the all surpassing power is from God and not from us. We are troubled on every side but not in distress, we are perplexed but not in despair, persecuted but not forsaken, and castdown but not destroyed.

SAFE IN THE ARMS OF JESUS

When we accept Jesus as our Savior, He not only provides for all our needs, but when we surrender our lives to Him and He indwells us, then He enables us to see the needs in the lives of those around us. When you pass the lonely or brokenhearted on the street or visit one who is critically ill, you can feel Him calling out to you to help that one in need.

Jesus said, when you feed the hungry, visit the shut-in, take care of the sick, visit those in prison, clothe the naked, give water to those who are thirsty, you are actually doing it for Him. He said, "When you did it for the least of these you did it for me".

Every blessing the Lord gives us, He gives it to us to share, not to hoard for ourselves, and that includes spiritual, physical, material and financial blessings. The amazing thing is that when we share our blessings we get more, but when we try to hold on to them for ourselves many times we lose them. We should not only be willing to open our home, give of our time and ourselves, but we should also be ready always to give away our greatest gift.

We have the gift of Eternal Life and we need to be ready always to give that gift away.

Thank You Father for all Your wonderful gifts. Please help us to be ready and willing to share all our blessings with those that You bring into our lives. Help us to hear You when You call out to us to help that one in need and thank You Father, for the times that You allow us to share our blessings.

James 1:17 Every good and perfect gift is from above, coming down from the Father of the heavenly lights, who does not change like shifting shadows.

SAFE IN THE ARMS OF JESUS

I'm safe in the arms of my Jesus,
So, please, don't worry about me....
Since I've been redeemed by the blood of the Lamb,
His precious face is all I can see.

His reflection is all about me,
In all the faces passing me by.....
He reflects all the need and the heartbreak,
You can see Him in their eyes.

He calls out to us from every station in life,
From among the great and the small.....
Don't close your eyes, your ears or your heart,
But listen and obey His call.

For others don't have this security,
That we'll have for forever and a day.....
They haven't found their way to the Savior,
So, please, let's show them without delay.

For every good and perfect gift,
Comes down from our Father above.....
And we are given our gift, (it's Jesus)
To share and show His love.

So, if you know my Jesus,
I must beg of you today.....
Tell someone else about your gift,
And try your best to give it away.

1985

Mark 9:36 What good is it for a man to gain the whole world, yet forfeit his soul? Friend, if you know Jesus, you have the gift of salvation in Your possession, give it to everyone you meet!

BUNDLES OF JOY

Dear One, if you have been blessed by God the Father, with a precious family, whether you have one child or many, each one is a very special gift. When God gives us a child He is entrusting that unique being into our care for the first and most critical segment of their lives.

What we do with our gift is totally up to us. There are many people who never realize, that whatever they sow into the fertile soil of that child's life, is what they will reap. When people turn their precious gift over to the T.V. or computer, a nanny or daycare center to raise (so that they don't have to be bothered), the quality of life in the future is going to be altered for that little one.

In many couples today, both parents have to work, but in some instances the couple is trying to keep up with the Joneses, they could actually live on a lot less and the Mother could stay home and raise the children as I believe the Lord intended, but sadly material things are too important today. Quite often couples have their priorities misplaced, and the children are always the ones to suffer for it.

Many homes today watch too much T.V., or they are so over-involved in extra curricular activities with the children's school, sports, ballet, tap, etc., that they don't have time for family bible reading and prayer. I wonder what would benefit the children the most later on in life. These above mentioned activities are not wrong as long as there is a balance in the home that includes spiritual things. Most homes if they have to let something take a back seat, sadly you can be sure it will be the Lord and the spiritual aspect of things in the family. Not only do our children need that good old spiritual food, just like we do, but it gives families some quality time together. With all the worldly distractions that seem to have popped up in most homes, there is very little family time. People today even eat their meals either on the run or in front of the T.V. set, and mealtime used to be a wonderful time for families to communicate.

So, saint of God, if the Lord has blessed you with a family... with precious little ones, please make their upbringing your most urgent priority, for always remember, we reap what we sow.

Proverbs 22: 6 Train a child up in the way he should go and when he is old he will not turn from it.

BUNDLES OF JOY

Babies are a gift from God,
Sent from heaven above…..
To shower with hugs and kisses,
And bushels and pecks of love.

They come in many different shapes and sizes,
As little bundles of joy…..
And you find when they arrive,
It really doesn't matter…if it's a girl or a boy.

They come in all colors,
Black, white, red…yellow and brown…..
But each one is God's own personal way,
Of spreading His love around.

You can take your gift,
And mold and make it as you choose…..
Or you can let God do the molding,
And then Your gift you won't misuse.

For only the Creator… really knows,
That special little one…..
And what it will take to mold them,
Into the image of His own Dear Son.

So, hand them over to the Master,
From *their* first day to *your* last…..
Then when it's time for you to go home,
You'll have no regrets from the past.

1985

Proverbs 20:7 The righteous man leads a blameless life; blessed are his children after him.

IS SOMETHING MISSING FROM YOUR LIFE?

Have you ever had a time in your life when everything seemed to be going wrong and for some reason you just couldn't put your finger on what was the matter or what had happened to cause you to feel like life was just not right? I think we all go through slumps, but then there are times that we feel like everything that can go wrong has or will.

Maybe you've had a lingering illness, lost your job or your marriage has fallen apart, and you've done everything you possibly can to try to understand why these things are happening to you. You've read and reread your Bible and listened to as many preachers on T.V. as you've had time to listen to; and yet nothing seems to do any good.

Dear One, you need to sit back and relax and let go and let God. Sometimes we allow ourselves to become so busy in all our Christian endeavors, that it doesn't leave us enough time to simply talk to the Lord, and then to wait for Him to speak. Not in an audible voice but by the Holy Spirit working through a friend, or simply that still small voice that the Holy Spirit sometimes uses. Or it can be the Holy Spirit impressing a particular passage of scripture on our hearts and we know it's the Lord speaking to us.

We must learn to rest in the Lord and quit trying to figure things out on our own. And we certainly can't fix things on our own either. Our Father wants us to cast all our cares on Him and to leave them there. In Proverbs 3:5-6 it says, Trust in the Lord with all your Heart and lean not on your own understanding, in all your ways acknowledge Him and He will direct your paths.

Our Father doesn't want us trying to figure out what's going on or why, He wants us to trust Him and He will carry us through the circumstance. He has not promised to remove all our trials but He has promised to see us through them. We can rest in the fact that as it says in Psalm 23, Ye, though I walk through the valley of The shadow of death, thou art with me. Well, child of God, the Lord Is with us wherever we go and whatever we go through.

Get your mind off yourself and your circumstances and get it on Jesus, and soon you'll find everything's going to be alright.

Peace and Rest come… with Trusting Jesus to see us through our trials.

IS SOMETHING MISSING FROM YOUR LIFE?

Do you feel that lately…
Something's missing from your life?
Do you feel your days are filled,
With too much heartache, sin and strife?

Does it seem like all you do,
Is think about your sorrow?
You worry about today…..
And then yesterday and tomorrow.

Your poverty and loss …
Are about to get you down,
You find you've lost your smile,
And it's nowhere to be found.

Perhaps it's been an illness,
That's lingered on too long…
It's left you feeling weak,
Where you once felt, oh, so strong.

Has the sorrow of losing a loved one,
left you spent in body and soul…
you feel your heart is broken,
and you're about to lose control?

You study and study your Bible…..
Looking for answers you just can't find,
And no matter where you look,
You find no peace of mind.

Perhaps you're working too hard,
Trying to study the Word…..
When in fact you've studied so hard,
Your Father's voice you haven't heard.

So just relax a little,
And go to God in prayer…..
Leave your sorrows and your heartaches,
Completely in 'His' care.

IS SOMETHING MISSING FROM YOUR LIFE? *Continued...*

Forget your labors and go to Jesus,
And rest in Him alone.....
Rest in the arms of the Savior,
At the foot of the Master's throne.

Get your mind off all your problems,
And on the Lord above.....
Then soon you'll find your cares replaced
By His matchless Grace and Love.

1985

Dear One, get your mind off self and get it on Jesus!

HAVE WE COME SO FAR THAT WE'VE FORGOTTEN?

Dear child of God, Have We Come So Far That We've Forgotten? Have we forgotten what it was like before we found the Lord? Have we forgotten what it was like when we didn't have our Father to share all our innermost thoughts and deepest feelings with, and to give all our heavy burdens to when we just can't carry them alone?

If we haven't forgotten, then why aren't we telling more people about Jesus? If we knew we had the cure for cancer and we saw people everywhere dying of cancer but refusing to take the shot because they were afraid of needles, I hope we would hit them over the head and knock them out if we had to, in order to save their lives. Well, we should feel the same way about people who are dying and going to hell without Jesus. We have their cure for everything and yet we don't tell them about it. Sometimes we don't want to put ourselves out and then sometimes we're afraid of what people might think of us.

We should be more concerned about people dying and going to hell than we are about what people think or anything else for that matter.

So, Dear One, please don't forget what it was like before you knew the Savior and take the time to share your blessing today.

Let's be like Paul, who said in II Timothy 2:8-9 Remember Jesus Christ, raised from the dead, descended from David. This is my gospel, for which I am suffering even to the point of being chained like a criminal. But God's word is not chained. Therefore I endure everything for the sake of the elect, that they too may obtain the salvation that is in Christ Jesus, with eternal glory.

HAVE WE COME SO FAR THAT WE'VE FORGOTTEN?

Is it day after day,
The same old grind.....
Until you think...one of these days,
You'll go out of your mind?

Life is such a rat race.....
And it seems you're getting nowhere.
As for happiness and joy,
You must have lost them somewhere.

When and where does it all end...
Do I have to die to find some peace?
But is death itself just darkness.....
And nothingness that will never cease?

There has to be an answer.....
But I wonder where it's found?
It's found in people like you and me,
When we spread God's love around.

When we give the lost the Gospel,
And new direction for their life.....
It's finding true salvation.....
From their heartache, sin and strife.

Have we come so far that we've forgotten,
What it was like before.....
When we didn't know the Savior,
And what He had in store?

Let's remember the questions we had,
Before our salvation day.....
The lost and lonely feelings,
Before we found our way.

So when that lost one passes by,
Don't let him get out of sight.....
But gently point the way,
From the darkness to the light.

HAVE WE COME SO FAR THAT WE'VE FORGOTTEN? *Continued...*

Tell him that Jesus loves him,
That He died to pay for his sin and strife.....
There's only one way to heaven...it's Jesus,
He's the Way, the Truth and the Life.

You'll never know peace on earth,
Or the joy of heaven sublime.....
Unless you take Jesus as your Savior,
Just as I took Him for mine.

Friend, don't forget what
it was like when you didn't
know Jesus.

1985

YOU SHALL LIGHT MY CANDLE

When we think we just can't make it our God is there, and He keeps us going. When we think we can't go on another day, He will see us through to the next day and the next, until it's time for our days to come to an end. When we think we can't make it another mile along our way, He will pick us up and carry us to the end of our journey.

Our Father lights our candle at the moment of our spiritual birth and then the rest of our lives He keeps our candle burning for His glory. We are to be His light in this sin darkened world, and we should never hide our candle under a bushel, but we are to let it shine for all the world to see.

Our candles are kept burning by Jesus, and they are the spark of life in our lives, but when we go home to heaven we won't need our candles any more for He will be the light.

Matthew 5:14-16 You are the light of the world. A city on a hill cannot be hidden. Neither do people light a lamp and put it under a bowl. Instead they put it on its stand, and it gives light to everyone in the house. In the same way, let your light shine before men, that they may see your good deeds and praise your Father in Heaven.

YOU SHALL LIGHT MY CANDLE

Lord,

You shall light my candle,
In the darkest hour of night…..
And keep my candle burning,
Not by mine…but by Your might.

And as my candle burns,
It turns my night to day…..
It brightens up my path,
And helps me find my way.

Then when my candle flickers,
In the lateness of the hour…..
You'll keep my candle burning,
Not by mine…but by Your power.

In the end, Father God,
When I take my last breath…..
my candle burns out
And my eyes close in death…

You'll be my candle,
And never leave me alone…....
For You promised You'd take me,
All the way home.

April 7, 1986

John 1:9 The true light that gives light to every man was coming into the world.

RELIGION IN A BOX

The poem RELIGION IN A BOX was written because a dear friend, Tim Smith, happened to mention during a conversation that some people act like their religion's in a box...and they do. Well, it made me think about it and sure enough I thought of how many people act as though God is a genie in a box and the only time they pull out the box is when they need something.

Many people who are in church every Sunday, their religion is in vain, for they don't even know what true religion is. And they only pull out their Religion in a Box when they want people to think they're Christians. Religion has given Christianity a bad name. So many bad things have been done in the name of religion. Besides, Christianity is not a religion it's a relationship. Many of these people are believers in the Lord Jesus Christ, and some may have even started out on the right foot, but somewhere along the line they got sidetracked and their religion got put in a box, and then the box got put on the shelf. They only pull it out when they have nothing else to do and they want to examine the box or when they need something and have nowhere else to turn.

Lord, help these people see they have lost their focus and they need to rebound and get back moving with Jesus. There may be times we all put You or our religion(relationship) in a box and put You briefly on the shelf, but I pray that will never happen, and if that process ever starts, make us keenly aware of what is about to happen, and help us not to make that serious mistake in judgment.

We love You Father, and we thank You for Your faithfulness, even when we're not faithful.

RELIGION IN A BOX

If you stop and think about it,
Don't you think it seems quite odd.....
That so many that call themselves believers,
Act as if they don't know God.

They may go to church on Sundays,
And sit quietly in their pew.....
But they hardly ever make a sound,
And they never learn anything new.

When people like that leave the building,
They go on with life just as before.....
Nothing they ever hear from the pulpit,
Seems to make any difference anymore.

Years ago they may have started out with Jesus,
But soon they let the ways of the world creep in.....
And all during the week they act,
As if nothing they do is a sin.

They never take time out for prayer,
And they never bother reading the Word.....
If the Holy Spirit whispered right in their ear,
They'd probably act as if they'd never heard.

When they need help or a shoulder to cry on,
The first thing they want to do... is tell God what it's all about.....
It's as if they have their religion in a box,
And suddenly... they want to take off the lid and pull it out.

They take the box off the shelf...just when necessary,
And take out just enough religion...... to get by this one time....
And then the box goes back on the shelf until later,
With a sign that says, "this box is mine".

It's such a shame more people don't understand,
That God is not just for special occasions ....
He wants to be involved in every moment of their lives,
Their sorrow and pain, laughter and tears and even their
Celebrations.

So let's recommend they empty out their box of religion,
And replace it with Jesus, the Spirit and the Word.....
Then the next time they hear that still small voice whispering,
There'll be no pretending that they just haven't heard.

James 1:22-25 Do not merely listen to the word, and so deceive yourselves. Do what it says. Anyone who listens to the word but does not do what it says is like a man who looks at his face in a mirror and, after looking at himself, goes away and immediately forgets what he looks like. But the man who looks intently into the perfect law that gives freedom, and continues to do this, not forgetting what he has heard, but doing it – he will be blessed in what he does.

CHRISTMAS HUSTLE BUSTLE

Dear Saint of God, Christmas has become so commercialized and hectic, that the real meaning of Christmas has somehow slipped away.

Even little children today, are so concerned about what they are going to be receiving from Santa, that they forget about why they are receiving anything at all. So many little ones know who they think Santa is but many probably couldn't tell you that Christmas is Jesus' birthday.

The world needs to get back to the basics, and to get it's priorities in order. It's not the gift giving and the celebrating with family and friends that are wrong, it's the fact that the world has forgotten why and what we're celebrating.

We should be rejoicing over the fact, that our SAVIOR was born into this world, to live a sinless life, and to be our sacrifice, so that we could spend Eternity in heaven. What a fantastic reason to celebrate. We are to give our gifts as if we are placing them at Jesus feet. We give them in His name, and with our utmost gratitude and thanksgiving for the Gift He has already given to us. We should want to be passing our gift along with love and joy that we have the ability to give.

Remember, Dear One, we could never out give God the Father, who not only gave us the gift of His Son, but He freely gives us so many other gifts as well. So from now on during the season of Christmas, let's let the world know what Christmas is all about, and never let the world around us take Christ out of Christmas for without Jesus there would be no Christmas.

CHRISTMAS HUSTLE BUSTLE

Hustle, bustle everywhere,
People rushing here and there…..
Package wrapping, flowers and bows,
Everyone rushing…where, who knows.

Parties and fun with family and friends,
When will all the rushing end?
Balls and tinsel adorn the tree,
Beneath sits the sweet Nativity.

Little Baby Jesus in the hay…..
But no one notices this Christmas Day.

Born to die so man might live,
Eternal life He freely gives.

God gave us the gift of His precious Son,
So easily we forget we're having too much fun!

2004

Jesus is the reason for the season. It's HIS BIRTHDAY, remember!

SOMETIMES I DON'T FEEL SAVED

Dear One, have you ever had a time in your Christian life when for some unexplained reason you felt like you might not be saved? You had thoughts like, what if I'm the only one who's not good enough to be saved, or what if all this is just some kind of story and none of it's for real, or I pray and pray but I never feel like my prayers are being heard? Or perhaps you've done something that you feel just wasn't covered by the blood of Jesus, so you must have lost your salvation.

There may come times in your life that you'll think you couldn't possibly be saved or you wouldn't have said, done or thought some particular thing. And that is exactly what the devil wants us to think. He wants us to believe that we're not good enough to be saved. But praise God our salvation doesn't depend on us it was paid for with Jesus blood, and that blood covers ALL our sin.

Thank you Father, that nothing can keep us out of heaven except our rejection of Your free gift of salvation. Even when we don't feel saved, we're still saved. So the next time the devil whispers in your ear that you can't be saved and have done, said or thought what you did, just say, "Get thee behind me Satan, Jesus did it all for me and I belong to the King of Kings and the Lord of Lords, and you can never have me!"

Salvation is not based on our feelings it's based on what Jesus did for us on the cross. Salvation is not a feeling it's a fact.

I John 5:13 These things I have written unto you who believe in the name of the Son of God, so that you may KNOW that you have eternal life.

SOMETIMES I DON'T FEEL SAVED

I don't always feel saved, Lord,
On some days that come and go.....
But salvation's not a feeling,
It's a fact that I can know.

For You tell me in Your Word,
I can know that I have eternal life.....
And with Your death on the cross,
You paid for all my sin and strife.

But there are times, and certain seasons, as the days go passing by.....
I feel kind of lost and lonely,
And I really don't know why.

Maybe it's just the devil,
trying to get me down.....
You know He's good at taking smiles,
And turning them into frowns.

Whatever it is Lord,
I give it all to you.....
And ask You Heavenly Father,
To help me make it through.

Through the times of worry and doubting,
Through the times of deep distress.....
Hide me in the shadow of Your wings,
And give me Your perfect peace and rest.

1985

I John 5:13I write these things to you who believe in the name of the Son of God, so that you may know that you have eternal life.

IT'S OVER

It's Over is a poem that I wrote when the precious young man Vinnie, who had been very ill for a long time, finally went home to be with the Lord. Vinnie and Robin his wife, went to our church and Vinnie was already ill when I moved to Atlanta and started going to the church. I heard about his illness and all the suffering he had been going through and had immediately begun praying for him and for his family.

I so hoped that the Lord would heal Vinnie, the way that we all wanted him to be healed. But our Father chose to heal him with the ultimate healing of taking him home to heaven to be with Him.

It has been such a privilege to get to know his wife Robin and to have the opportunity to meet Vinnie before the Lord took him home.

I wrote this poem as, hopefully, an opportunity to lift Robin's spirits. It's very difficult to lose someone you love especially at a young age, but I know Vinnie would say these things to Robin if he could.

God Bless You and Your Family, Robin,

IT'S OVER

Dear ones at last it's over,
My suffering and pain are now no more.....
Jesus, friends and loved ones were waiting,
When at last I stepped on shore.

I love you and hated to leave you,
But absolutely nothing could be so grand.....
As being shown all around God's heaven,
While holding our Savior's hand.

How could we have ever imagined,
Gates of pearl and streets paved with gold.....
Eye has not seen nor ear heard,
Nor the real story ever been told.

For no words could ever really describe it,
The awesome majesty and beauty everywhere.....
But as overwhelming as it is, there's nothing like Jesus,
And being in His...loving care.

So dear ones, I'll definitely see you later,
And I can't wait until at last I see your face.....
I'll be waiting at the finish line with the saints and angels,
Shouting hallelujah as you finish your race.

It's okay to cry a few tears, but rejoice!
For don't forget we'll be together for forever come what may.....
So, until I see you at the gates of glory,
Don't forget I love you... and I'll see you on your homecoming day.

January 2006

As it is written: "Eye has not seen nor ear heard neither has entered into the heart of man the things that God has prepared for those who love Him." But God has revealed it unto us by His Spirit. The Spirit searches all things, even the deep things of God. I Cor. 2:9-10

DEAR, HURTING ONES

"Dear, Hurting Ones" is a poem written way back in 1985 and yet it is so appropriate for today. Having been in the cemetery and funeral home business for the last 21 years, I have dealt with so many grieving families, and I want so much to be able to make things a little better for them during their time of need.

I want the families to know, that if I am able to be any encouragement whatsoever, that it is really not me, but Jesus loving or ministering through me, and to give Him the praise and thanks, not me. I have no merit of my own.

Jesus left us a comforter when He went to heaven, in the form of the Holy Spirit. The Holy Spirit will not only comfort God's children, but He will lead us and guide us in all that we do, if we'll let Him. But He will most certainly lead and guide us into all truth, and God's truth is what will see families through the loss of a Loved one or a friend. His truth will light our way in the darkest hour of night.

So, Dear, Hurting Ones, let God's Holy Spirit lead you into all truth and the truth will minister to you in a very special way, for in the beginning was the word and the Word was with God and the word was God. So, that tells me that Jesus is the Word and when we read the Word we are allowing Jesus to minister to us. Read John 1:1.

Let God love you through His Word!

II Cor.1:3-4 Blessed be God, the Father of mercies and the God of all comfort, who comforts us in all our tribulations, so that we can comfort them who are in any trouble with the same comfort by which we ourselves are comforted of God.

DEAR HURTING ONES

No words could ever express,
The deep feelings in my heart.....
And if I could find the words,
I still wouldn't know where to start.

So I'll just say I care,
And I know you won't lose sight.....
Of the fact that Joy comes in the morning,
Weeping only lasts for the night.

I'm only a tool in the hands of Jesus,
My own ability is, oh, so small.....
And any comfort I might bring,
Doesn't come from me at all.

For only God can mend our hearts,
When we think they're broken beyond repair.....
And He promises in His word,
All sufficient grace, love and care.

So, just for now, you know the place,
Where you can run and hide.....
Straight to our precious Savior,
With His arms held open wide.

And in this hour of need,
Take refuge in the shadow of His wings.....
And when the morning comes,
You'll find your heart still sings.

God Can and Will Bless You in Your hour of Need!

1985

Psalms 30:5 Weeping may endure for the night but joy cometh in the morning.

Psalms 57:1-2 Have mercy on me oh, God, have mercy on me, for my soul trusteth in Thee, in the shadow of Thy wings will I take my refuge until all these calamities be passed by.

THE MASTER PAINTER

Sometimes I think of God as a painter and we are His work of art and other times I think of Him as a weaver at His loom and our lives are His tapestry.

It's as if all of nature is His canvas and He created this beautiful painting and the finishing touch in the painting was the life of man. To think that He would include unworthy sinners in His painting and yet He took the black of our sin and combined it with the Red of Jesus blood and it became purest white (our salvation).

Jesus painted the portrait for everyone who ever lived, and yet so many try to get their own canvas and paint their own painting, but they could never out paint the Master no matter how hard they tried.

Sadly when Jesus presents the finished painting of their lives in Him, many choose to look away and they will never know what their final finished painting would have looked like. How beautiful it would have been, and yet it was a wasted canvas, that had to be thrown into the fire.

Friend, Let Jesus include you in His painting, your artwork can't compare to His. Would you want a painting full of imperfections or would you prefer a perfect painting?

The choice is yours today, a flawless painting by the Master, or your own pitiful imitation, which one shall it be?

THE MASTER PAINTER

It just seems so amazing….that from Black and Green and Brown,
The Lord can paint a tree…and plant it in the ground.

He takes blue and white to make the sky… sometimes black and gray,
When instead of sunshine, He paints a cloudy day.

Now and then He'll paint some streaks….of Yellow, Green and Red…
As a beautiful reminder, of just what lies ahead.

He paints some pink in the evening sky, and in some of summer's blooms,
Painting canvases left and right…like a weaver at His loom.

Flowers of many colors blooming in the Spring…..
Leaves of Rust and Gold are painted in the Fall,
The world, the universe, a tiny baby –
Nothing seems too great…or too small.

For the brush stroke of the Master, who paints according to His will…
Until He calls us home at last, will keep on painting still.

Until the end of time He'll paint – but there's one thing,
We just can't comprehend….
How Red on Black turns purest White, when stirred in the Hearts of men.

The Red the Blood, the Black our sin, the White So Great Salvation…
Painted by God's precious Son, for every tribe and nation.

Some will never see the painting…sadly they turned and looked away,
And now when Jesus calls us home…they'll miss that glorious day.

1988

Isaiah 1:18 Though your sins are like scarlet, they shall be as white as snow, though they are red as crimson, they shall be like wool.

MY BURIED TREASURE

The poem "My Buried Treasure" was written as a reminder to my families that I deal with in the cemetery business, that when we have a wonderful godly mate that we've been married to for many years, and they go home to be with the Lord, we must remember that they were always a special gift from God the Father.

We can be so thankful for the time that we were allotted with our spouse, and we can know that they were given to us as our own special treasure. And our Father in His amazing grace blessed us with that treasure for eternity. It's not as if we will never see them again, because we will. They will be waiting for us when we ourselves are called home to glory. It's only a shell or tent that is waiting in the grave. And someday when the Rapture takes place, all those who have already gone home to be with the Lord will be coming back and reinhabiting their tent, and that tent will become a new glorified body. All those who are still alive at the time of the Rapture will be taken up into heaven at the same moment as those who are reinhabiting their tents (bodies).

What a great time to look forward to. We will not only be with our Heavenly Father, but with all those that we knew and loved, who had already gone before. Our Buried Treasure will no longer be buried, but will instead be reunited with us in heaven. What a glorious reunion!

Thank you Father for the special treasures that You give us so graciously, help us to be mindful of how priceless they are and how truly wonderful You are.

MY BURIED TREASURE

I had a special treasure,
It was given to me by God…..
And now my treasure rests,
Beneath the cold, cold sod.

But nothing could ever replace,
What the Lord gave me long ago…..
And before he left for heaven,
I always tried to let him know…..

Just how very much I loved him,
And that no other could take his place…..
For we were brought together by God,
And His amazing grace.

Although my treasure's buried,
His spirit waits in glory…..
The place we'd always heard about,
In god's own special story.

Then one day my treasure,
Will be raised up from the ground…..
For we'll be leaving this old earth,
And we'll both be heavenward bound.

So, yes, my treasure may be buried,
But just for a short time…..
And whether up in heaven or on earth,
This treasure is mine all mine.

2006

THE LESSON OF LOVE

We can be a genuinely good person and in fact we may love and care about many people, but I don't believe we can unconditionally love everyone, (especially the most unlovely) apart from Jesus loving them through us.

We want our Father God to love us unconditionally and in spite of our sin and yet we don't want to love others the same way. We only love the people we choose to love. We want everyone to love us and when someone doesn't we just can't understand how they could possibly not love "us". We pick and choose people to whom we will give our love. You know the Lord's prayer says, "forgive us our trespasses as we forgive those who trespass against us." What if it said, "Love us as we love others" the very thought should convict us.

Surrendering all to Jesus just makes sense, for whenever we let Him live in and through us it enables us to love everyone, including the unlovely. We can let Him do for us, whatever we are incapable of doing for ourselves. Isn't that absolutely the greatest? I think so!

THE LESSON OF LOVE

In this life we're given to live,
During our years upon this earth…..
We're given one lesson to master,
From the day of our new birth.

The lesson is set before us,
"Thou shalt love…as I have loved you"…..
and we must learn to apply the lesson,
in all that we say and do.

For unless we master the lesson of love,
While living here below…..
We'll miss the joy of living…
No matter what we know.

In the midst of all our duties, cares and trials,
Sorrows and joys of each day…..
Unless we have learned the art of loving,
We have somehow lost our way.

For the most important commandment,
That we must learn to obey…….
Is to unconditionally love the ones,
From whom we'd turn away

They may possess every characteristic,
We detest or just don't understand…..
But Jesus says, "Love them for my sake".
So reach out and offer a hand.

Our Father loves us so very much,
No less then we should do……
And if we've mastered the lesson of love,
We'll be able to love the unlovely too.

1985

…we love because He first loved us. I John 4:19

YESTERDAY, TODAY AND TOMORROW

So many people spend their days worrying about what happened yesterday, or what might happen tomorrow, that before they know it their today has passed them by and instead of using it productively for the Lord, they wasted it worrying about the past that they can't change and about things that might happen tomorrow and yet they may not happen.

We must live one day at a time and use each day as if it were our last. Let the Lord live through us each day and use us to be a blessing to all the people we come in contact with.

The devil does his best to keep us from being productive Christians and so many of us let him have the victory. Christian, stand your ground and don't let him have the victory for Jesus has already fought and won the battle if we will only claim the victory. Remember the battle's already been won. Jesus is the Victor! So Christian walk victoriously!

We have someone to fight our battles for us who will always win, so why do we try to do the fighting? Surrender your all to Jesus today and rest while He fights the battles for you.

Victory in Jesus!

YESTERDAY, TODAY AND TOMORROW

Yesterday is gone now,
We cannot live it another way.....
So we must try to forget the past,
And let God use today.

The sorrow of yesterday remembered,
Only serves to bring us grief.....
The joys of yesterday.....should be,
Only a sweet relief.

Tomorrow....is out of our hands,
So why worry about what we can't see?
We think we have something to worry about,
But that something may never be.

And when we spend today worrying,
About yesterday or tomorrow......
We waste our precious day,
Filling it with fear and sorrow.

The fear of what might be tomorrow,
And sorrow over what happened yesterday....
Can only serve to waste the time,
God has given us for today.

It's true we should learn from yesterday,
And have high hopes for tomorrow....
But from the past and the future,
It's best that we never borrow.

Today is very special,
And it comes to us only one time.....
So we must try to remember,
This day is really His not mine.

Each day is like a stepping stone,
Leading up a path to glory.....
At the end of the path a mansion awaits,
For all who've believed the story.

YESTERDAY, TODAY AND TOMORROW
Continued...

So let's not take our eyes from the pathway,
To look back at old yesterday…..
For if we look back for too long,
We might find ourselves going astray.

And if we look too far ahead,
Instead of at each stone,
We may look up and one day find……
We're walking all alone.

So ask the Lord to give us…His grace…
…just enough for today…..
Knowing when tomorrow comes,
He'll be with us in the very same way.

1985

One step at a time sweet Jesus!

I'm A Know-So

I'm a Know-So is a poem I wrote to remind us of how important it is to know where we're going when we die. Not only does it give us peace of mind, but you can't give others any real hope or peace of mind, if you don't have any real hope or peace of mind yourself.

I have always loved the scripture in I John 5:13 that says, I write these things to you who believe in the name of the Son of God, that you may know that you have eternal life. What more do we need than that? It doesn't say we can hope that we have eternal life, or we can believe or think that we have eternal life, it says we can KNOW.

I'm sure our Father knew that there would be times that the devil would whisper things in our ear in order to get us to question or doubt our salvation, but all we have to do is read or quote that scripture and it can restore our faith and peace. It's good to have that particular scripture memorized in case the devil chooses to attack when we don't have a Bible handy. The Lord quoted the scriptures at Satan, when he was tempted up on the mount. In fact the word is alive, and quick and powerful and sharper than any two-edged sword. In other words it's POW ER FUL!

Friend be a Know-So! And show others how they can be a Know-So too.

I'M A KNOW-SO

I'm so glad that I'm a Know-so... not a hope-so,
When it comes to my salvation.....
And that I've put my faith and trust in Jesus,
And not some spiritual evaluation.

Praise God, my sins have all been forgiven,
And my home awaits in glory.....
My citizenship's in heaven,
Just like it says in the old, old story.

At last I've been set free,
I've passed from death to life.....
Now I can live forever,
For my Jesus paid the price.

With His blood He paid the price,
For all my sin and shame......
Oh, glory hallelujah,
Praise His holy name.

My faith is all in Christ,
I have no merit of my own.....
The only righteousness that I have,
Well, it comes from Him alone.

In heaven there'll be no religions,
No labels with strange sounding names......
We'll all simply be God's children,
No more playing religious games.

We'll be one big family in heaven,
Surrounding our Father's throne.....
Living in the light of His glory and love,
And, so, thankful at last to be home.

June 26, 1985

I John 5:13 I write these things to you who believe in the name of the Son of God, so that you may know that you have eternal life.

SLOWDOWN AND REMEMBER

It's seems strange that so often people have their lives upside down and backwards. The things that are not really that important in life seem to be their priority and the things that really matter the most take a backseat. It's not always that they don't realize that these things are important, it's just that they don't seem as important as they really are.

What's more important, helping a neighbor in need or cleaning my house? Helping someone in need or mowing the yard? I have found in my own life if I put the needs of others first, then the Lord will take care of my needs. In Philippians 2:3-4 it says, Do nothing out of selfish ambition or vain conceit, but in humility consider others better than yourselves. Each of you should look not only to your own interests but also to the interests of others.

We need to remember to store up our treasures in heaven, where moth and rust don't corrupt, instead of on earth. We need to be more heavenly minded. When we put others first, we seem to find our joy in wonderful ways and it's a kind of joy that nothing in the world has to offer. God so richly blesses us when we put the needs of others above our own, that once that becomes a habit, we can't wait for new opportunities to serve or minister to others.

Dear One, SLOWDOWN AND REMEMBER!

SLOWDOWN AND REMEMBER

Did I remember to say "I love you",
When I started off my day?
Or did I start in such a hurry,
That I just went the other way?

Small things that are so important,
We often forget about in our rush.....
Big things that are so trivial,
We've got to do it or bust.

Do we have our lives in order,
And do the things that really count?
Or does the stack of good deeds...left undone,
Suddenly seem to mount?

We may not have tomorrow to say I love you...
Or to say, please forgive....
So let's use each day, as if it were.....
The last we had to live.

Forgetting all the wrongs and,
Letting others know we care.....
Not simply in words alone,
But we should also offer to share.

For offering to share their burdens,
Can often set a lighter tone.....
And nothing seems quite as heavy,
When you don't have to go it alone.

It's such a simple thing,
To say I love you to one another.....
To slip our arms around and hug,
That sister or that brother.

But how it lifts us up,
When we've slipped into despair.....
To have a precious friend in Christ,
Let us know they care.

God blesses us in many ways,
Just to show His love.....
Sometimes through a friend,
Or through an angel from above.

So, let's slow down and remember,
The things that seem so big.....
Are really, oh, so small,
And we can do some little things....
To replace the biggest one of them all.

A hug, a kiss, a pat on the back,
The loving touch of a hand.....
If we "Slowdown and Remember",
Can say, "I care and understand.".

2006

IT WAS SUCH A SMALL THING

It can be Such a Small Thing, that can destroy a life, a marriage, a family, a church or even our world. One little tiny match can be the thing that lights an uncontrollable forest fire, that not only destroys the forest, but it may kill animals and people and burn down hundreds of homes, causing terrific devastation.

The tongue is such a small member of the body, and yet just one little word spoken out of place or in the wrong tone of voice, can lead to fussing and fighting and things we may regret.

Children left to themselves can grow up to be who knows what.

Flirting with temptation can only lead to heartbreak for someone.

We must have God as our foundation, in our home, marriage, friendship and working relationships. He is our security.

"It Was Such A Small Thing" was one of only two non- rhyming poems that I have written so far but I know the Lord gave it to me for a reason and I had to be obedient and write it down.

Perhaps it well encourage some teenager to make a right decision or some child of God, about to get caught up in the wrong thing, to make the right choice.

One small thing can lead to such big things, dear one, keep God in the center of the big things and the small things and you can never lose.

It's Such a Small Thing, but it may not be so small after all.

Dear One, may God Give you the wisdom and strength to make right choices and decisions in all that you do.

IT WAS SUCH A SMALL THING

I always wondered:

Why did God deal so harshly
With Moses His servant,
Just for smiting the rock?
It was such a small thing.

What's the harm done by a few cutting words
Aimed at someone you love?
They'll understand.... you've had a hard day.
It's such a small thing.

One little drink just to relax,
With a friend from work.....
After all he needed cheering up!
It's such a small thing.

All the little boys do it.....
They just take a little peek,
And besides all the stores sell them.
What's the harm...it's such a small thing?

Just one date.
So he's an unbeliever.
Well he might even come to know the Lord later.
It's no big deal, it's such a small thing.

Cutting remarks can leave permanent scars.....
And one drink can lead to another and another and another....
Those sweet little boys can grow into rapist or worse.
And just one date with an unbeliever can lead to a bad
Marriage, divorce or an illicit affair.
But you know....after all these were such small things.

1985

I Peter 1:14-15 As obedient children, do not conform to the evil desires you had when you lived in ignorance. But just as He who called you is holy, so be holy in all you do.

Romans 12:2 Do not conform to this world but be transformed by the renewing of your minds.

COME HOME

Friend, if you've been wandering around in darkness and you're ready to get back to the light, don't put it off. We are not guaranteed another tomorrow so we can't waste any time procrastinating. This is a very serious matter. Not because we will lose our salvation but do we really want Jesus to come back and find us living out in the world like an unbeliever?

I don't think I'd want my Savior to come back and find me living out in the world and it's ways. Besides a Christian can't ever be really happy living in the world out of fellowship with the Lord. We're only happy when we're living the life our Father meant for us to live. Joy is not the absence of suffering but the presence of God in our lives.

Christians are one body and when any part of the body isn't functioning properly then the body is not working like it should and could be. It will cause the rest of the body to be trying to compensate for the missing part. Just like when a person has a part of their body,(Leg, arm, etc.) missing, it will learn to compensate for the missing part but it will never be the same as when the body was whole and in good working order.

Dear one, if you are wandering around out there somewhere, please, come home soon, we miss you. Things are just not the same without you.

COME HOME

It's never too late to turn back to the Lord…..
Whether you're eighteen or eighty…one hundred or ten.
He's waiting to receive you…with arms open wide…
Back into the family again.

He never remembers the times in your past…..
They're forgotten to Him for always.
He only cares that His precious child,
Who once strayed….has come home to stay.

If you'll turn around right where you are…..
You'll find Jesus...leading the way.
The way back to joy and fellowship sweet…..
The way back from night into day.

You may have spent years…many years,
Living in the very vilest of sins…..
But the past won't matter one bit, my friend,
When your brand new life begins.

His voice is ever calling you,
Come back to your family and friends…..
You've been gone quite awhile,
But you'll be back forever…and forever never ends.

Don't waste another minute,
Living out there on your own…..
But turnaround…take His hand,
And let Him lead you back home.

The angels will be singing,
And shouting with great joy…..
Over the long awaited return,
Of that lost man, woman…..girl or boy.

With even one child missing,
The family's really just not complete…..
Songs don't ring as loudly,
Fellowships just not quite as sweet.

COME HOME Continued...

So, please come home, my friend,
Don't dare try to delay.....
Tomorrow may never come,
So, come right away.

Because he loves you and we miss you.....
Hurry Home!

2006

I John 1:9 If we confess our sins, He is faithful and just to forgive us of our sins and to cleanse us from all unrighteousness.

I TAKE THE BLAME

I Take the Blame is a poem I wrote trying to encourage believers to admit and confess their sins. Many people never bother to keep their sins confessed and so they stay out of fellowship. Unfortunately when we have any unconfessed sin in our lives the Lord doesn't hear our prayers.

Some people say, "Father forgive me for my many sins", when they start to pray, (which may or my not be very frequently) and that's just taking the easy way out.

The Lord wants us to name our sins, so that He knows, that we know and admit what we have done. Just as at times, we want our own children to own up to what they have done. It cleans the slate and gives us a contrite heart.

It's always best to confess our sins immediately as soon as we realize that we have committed one. For until we confess the sin, we will remain out of fellowship with the Lord. We need to ask the Lord to have the Holy Spirit convict us of any sin that's in our lives, and to help us to respond to that conviction.

It's a humbling experience to admit your sin before a Holy God and yet it is extremely important, if you want to keep a right relationship with Him. Besides the scriptures say, "Humble yourself in the sight of the Lord and in due time He will lift you up. Being on your face before the Father is a great place to be for any believer. And we should be ready always to confess any sin that overtakes us, because we want our line of communication to remain open at all times.

I John 1:9 If we confess our sins, He is faithful and just to forgive us of our sins and to cleanse us from all unrighteousness.

Psalm 66:18 If I regard iniquity in my heart He will not hear me. My friend, keep your slate clean!

I TAKE THE BLAME

Guess what, it's me, Lord,
And at last I'm finally able to see…..
It's not any other,
It's just me.

For I used to think… when I sin,
I'm not the one to blame…..
Then I'd do my best…to avoid,
All the sorrow and the shame.

For in the past it was always so easy,
To shift the blame on to another…...
To some stranger or some friend,
Or even a sister or a brother.

To carry all the blame alone,
Well, it was just too rough…..
And sharing it at least,
Made it seem not quite as tough.

But Lord, You've finally reached,
That place deep within…..
Where I did my very best,
To conceal all my sin.

And now You've placed it all,
Right before my eyes…..
That ugliness and sin,
That I loath and despise.

Father, I now confess,
And I must take full blame…...
Because I don't want my life,
To ever be the same.

And every single sin,
That You can see in me…..
I must now own up to,
And admit wholeheartedly.

For I never want a barrier,
Between me and You…..
And I always want my prayers,
Easily…Able to get through.

2006

I John 1:9 If we confess our sins He is faithful and just to forgive us for our sins and to cleanse us from all unrighteousness.

AS WE SEE STRANGERS PASSING BY

When we see people passing us by do we avoid looking them in the eye, because we don't really want to know if they have a need? Or if they do have a need we don't want to have to get involved. Most people don't want to take time out of their schedules for others because that means they would have a little less time for themselves.

Actually, we are supposed to put the needs of others first and when we do the Lord takes care of our needs Himself. We are always to esteem others as more important than ourselves.

Our Father gives us the privilege of being His instruments, and we are blessed not only to be used by the God of the universe to do His will and to accomplish His plan, but we are abundantly blessed by Him when we do allow Him to use us. It's just incredible!

What an awesome God we serve!

We must never harden our hearts to the needs of those around us. We must always be sensitive to the needs of others, and ask our Father, to help us see everyone through His eyes and the way that He sees them. We must always respond to the prompting of the Holy Spirit.

Dear Lord, keep us sensitive!

AS WE SEE STRANGERS PASSING BY

As we see strangers passing by.....
Do we hear their heartfelt ...silent cry?
And do we see the sadness and longing on their face.....
Yet just pass them on by in life's hurried pace?

Are we the least bit affected by what we see,
Or do we only have the time to think of me?
It's so easy to "feel", for those who have a need.....
But it's another story to do a good deed.

Thinking and doing are two different things.....
Responding to the need, that's what makes the heart sing.
It not only blesses the one who's needs are met.....
But the doer of the deed is blessed too, you can bet!

The Lord sees all that we do...both day and night,
Even our motives are plain in His sight......
So when you see that someone truly has a need,
Let the Jesus in you, reach out and take the lead.

For when the Lord uses us ...to accomplish His will,
We find in all the earth, that there is no greater thrill.....
The knowledge...that God would even consider using me,
Is beyond imagination ...that He would let it be.

So, thank You, Father, for letting me be a vessel You can use.....
I'm amazed To think that I could ever be... the one that You would choose,
And then to allow me to feel the joy that it brings.....
Just to be a servant in the kingdom of the King.

1985

Dear One, what a thrill to be given the privilege of being a servant of the
King! Thank You, Father!

**Philippians 2:12 Therefore, my dear friends, as you have always
obeyed, not only in my presence, but now much more in my absence —
continue to work out your salvation with fear and trembling, for it is
God who works in you to will and to act according to His good purpose.**

HE'S ALWAYS THERE

Isn't it fantastic to know that we have a wonderful Savior, that willingly gave His life so that we could live forever in eternity with Him, and once we belong to Him, there is not a single place we can go that He won't be right there with us? Of course there may be times that some people wish He wouldn't be right there with them, for they may have gone somewhere, that they know they shouldn't have gone to begin with, or done something they know they shouldn't have done.

The great thing about knowing He's always there with us wherever we are, is that we can have peace regardless of our circumstances. When you know that you have God the Father and His Son, Jesus Christ, the Savior of the world with you at all times, what could we possibly have to fear or worry about?

There are so many lost and lonely people in the world and we need to have a tremendous burden for their souls. They not only need a Savior, but they also need a friend. So, tell everyone you meet about Jesus. And we can't find any excuse for not telling people. II Timothy 1:7 says, "For God has not given us a spirit of fear (or timidity), but of power, and of love and of a sound mind." If we think we aren't the type to try to talk to strangers about the Lord, if we really see them as dying and going to hell, if we really want to give them the opportunity to accept Christ as their Savior, all we have to do is ask the Lord, to do it Himself, through us, and He will. He's not willing that anyone should perish but that all should come to repentance.

We are blessed, above all people, if we know He's Always There!

Don't forget God Loves YOU!

HE'S ALWAYS THERE

Jesus never said in life,
That we wouldn't have the storms…..
But when the lightening flashes and the thunder crashes,
We'll be safe…in His loving arms.

For our faith was never founded,
On the sinking sands of time……
But on the solid Rock of Ages,
And that's why I'm doing fine.

Doing fine when all about me,
Is sorrow, grief and sadness…..
And although I'm sometimes weary,
My heart is filled with gladness.

Sadly so many lonely souls,
Are sinking down in deep despair…..
If only they'd "reachout"…..
And take hold of Jesus' love and care.

If they would simply turn around,
And grasp His precious hand…..
They'd find His grace is free to all,
And available on demand.

They'd see that He's never too busy,
In the tumult of the day…..
To give them new direction,
When they might have lost their way.

He's always ready to listen,
To our cry when we're in distress…..
Or to hear our shout of rejoicing,
Upon finding a place to rest.

Oh, the peace and comfort,
Of knowing my Jesus is always near…..
So the storms of life may rage about me,
But I'll have no need for fear.

HE'S ALWAYS THERE Continued...

And even if the mountains should crumble,
And fall into the midst of the sea…..
I'll never be afraid,
For I know…my Savior cares for me.

1985

Psalm 46:1-2 God is our refuge and strength, an ever-present help in trouble. Therefore we will not fear, though the Earth give way and the mountains fall into the heart of the sea.

IS YOUR HEART RIGHT?

Saint of God, have you ever had a time in your life when you probably couldn't put your finger on what was wrong, but you knew something just wasn't right in your life? Or perhaps you did know what was wrong, but you simply ignored the voice of the Holy Spirit when it tried to convict you. Well sadly, until you face the facts, and admit and confess what you've done, you are going to be out of fellowship with the Lord for that period of time. And when we are out of fellowship the Lord doesn't hear our prayers.

The funny thing is, some people delay or put off acknowledging or confessing their sins and then they wonder why they're miserable. You can't remain out of fellowship for any length of time and be happy. The Holy Spirit (thank God!) won't let you. But whether or not you listen to Him is up to you.

We all need to examine ourselves on a regular basis, and it's actually best if we confess our sin as soon as we realize we've committed one. That way we keep a clean slate between us and the Father. And we should never want anything to be between us. We shouldn't want anything to interrupt our relationship with the King of kings, for we are His servants and we always need to be fit for His service.

Be prepared at all times friend, so the Father can use you for His glory!

Psalm 66:18 If I regard iniquity in my heart He will not hear me.

Sin clogs up our pipeline to God and He can't hear us, but when we confess our sins, it's like ROTO ROOTER going through the pipeline and cleaning it out, so that He can hear us again.

IS YOUR HEART RIGHT?

When darkness suddenly falls,
Upon your once bright way......
And loneliness seems to follow you,
All through the day.......

...do you ever stop and take a minute,
to see if all's right inside.....
or because of circumstances,
do you just want to run and hide?

Sometimes... when everything in your life,
Seems to be going wrong.....
And you find tears and sadness have replaced,
Your happy heart's song.....

.....you need to take the time out to check....
And see if all's right within.....
for the problem just might be,
some unconfessesd sin.

For if you've been walking in the darkness,
And longing for the light.....
You must take a little time out to ask yourself,
"Is Your Heart Right?"

And if you find a little sin,
Has hidden itself deep inside.....
Simply turn to Jesus,
For to Him you can confide.

And once you confess to the Savior,
You'll know your heart's right.....
And you'll find yourself walking,
Right back in the light.

1985

I John 1:9 If we confess our sins He is faithful and just to forgive us of our sins and to cleanse us from all unrighteousness.

TIME IS SLIPPING AWAY

Dear One, do you realize that Jesus could come back today? This could literally be the day when we hear the trumpet sound and our feet suddenly leave the ground and we're out of here. Should we be going along acting as if this is just another day? There are souls that need saving today!

We happen to live in the most exciting time in Christian history. All the prophecy has been fulfilled that had to be fulfilled before Jesus was going to come back. We don't need to sit idly by, when there are still people who have either never accepted Christ, or they haven't even heard the Gospel story. It's our job, until Jesus does come back, to be reaping the harvest of souls. He told us the fields are white, ready for harvest. So, let's get busy people, and be ready when He comes again.

Everyone needs Jesus, and there may be those with whom we feel like we don't want to be bothered. In fact, because of who they are we may just feel like letting someone else reach out to that person, but our Father doesn't say love the lovely, or reach out when we feel like it. He expects us to love the unlovely and to offer the Gospel to any and everyone.

Everyday when you wake up just remember, this could be the day. So get to work and be ready, and hopefully you'll hear the Lord say, "Well done good and faithful servant", when He comes to take us home.

May the Lord bless you as you seek to reach the lost.

John 4:35-36 I tell you, open your eyes and look at the fields! They are ripe for harvest. Even now the reaper draws his wages, even now He harvests the crop for eternal life, so that the sower and the reaper may be glad together.

TIME IS SLIPPING AWAY

The time on the clock is ticking down,
that day will be here by and by.....
The day we leave this earth,
And meet our Jesus in the sky.

The time you have until He comes,
How will you use it, my friend.....
Will you use it to glorify His name,
Or to bring you to a hopeless end?

Have you put your faith and trust in the Savior,
And been given life anew.....
If not, please do it today,
For the end is almost in view.

The time is passing so quickly,
Each second is slipping away.....
And yet, with so much work to be done,
What will you do with today?

As the sands of time slip on down,
Through the hourglass of our days.....
Will we let the Lord lead by His Spirit,
Or push on in our own selfish ways?

When the last tick is tocked,
And the last grain of sand trickles down.....
What will you be doing,
And where will you be found?

1985

I Thessalonians 4:16-18 And the Lord Himself will descend from heaven with a shout and the voice of the archangel, and the trumpet call of God, and the dead in Christ shall rise first, and then we who are alive and remain shall be caught up together with them in the clouds to meet the Lord in the air, and so shall we ever be with the Lord, wherefore, comfort one another with these words.

A SPECIAL TOUCH FROM YOU

There have been times in my own life when I have felt down or discouraged and bewildered. I have even had times when I haven't known the reason for my feelings or why I happened to find myself in this low place, but I have always known that those are usually the times in my life when I need something special from my Lord.

Sometimes His special touch can come through the care and concern of a friend and at other times it might just be something that the Holy Spirit leads me to read in the Word. It might even be a particular song and it's wording that I'm listening to on the radio or on one of my own CDs, that happens to minister to me in a special way, right at the time when I need it the most. It's amazing how the Lord knows exactly what we need and when. He's aware of our every need and concern and He never fails to meet those needs and to take care of our concerns.

Many times I have been having my devotions and the very Psalm or passage of scripture that I'm reading from is exactly what I needed at that particular moment and the Lord directed me to those very words in order to meet a special need. Our God is so good!

Thank you, Father, for Your faithfulness in meeting our needs.

In His Name,

Carolyn

A SPECIAL TOUCH FROM YOU

Your word says You care…and I believe it,
Your word says You love me and I know it's true…..
But some days when I'm sad, lonely and brokenhearted,
Lord, I just need a special touch from You.

You're all that I want…You're all that I need,
You're my Father, Creator, Savior and Friend…..
You're my Rock of Ages, my Sure Foundation,
And I know You'll be with me right to the end.

But with all that You are to me…and ever will be,
Still there are times when I feel so lonesome and so blue…..
Knowing You care and yet I cry out in despair,
"Lord, I need to feel a special touch from You".

For I find nothing in this world can satisfy my soul,
Nothing else can mend this broken heart of mine…..
So, although I give in to fears, sadness…sometimes tears,
I still await Your precious touch divine.

For Your touch has…
The power to raise me when I'm feeling low,
The power to give me joy and sweet peace within…..
It has the power to save me and to take me home to glory,
It's that same power that saved me from my sin.

So regardless of my circumstances,
And the sorrow and pain that I may feel…..
I know that Your joy and peace await me,
For Your special touch is oh, so real.

February 6, 1987

Father, thank You so much, for Your special touch, and for all the joy and
peace it can bring, often just when we need it the most.

SATAN'S A SUBTLE SO AND SO

The devil is so powerful and we really don't give him credit where credit is due. The world, the flesh and the devil are always warring against us, and we must keep our armor on in order to fight the battle efficiently.

Saint of God, we must be ready for his attacks at all times. It is best to get up and first thing before you get out of bed, put on the whole armor of God. The breastplate of righteousness, the belt of truth, the helmet of salvation, take up the shield of faith, the sword of the spirit and shod our feet with the preparation of the gospel of peace.

I Peter says, "your adversary the devil, like a roaring lion stalks about seeking whom he may devour". Be ready, but also remember, that greater is He that is in you than he that is in the world.

The Scriptures say in Romans 8:38 that I am persuaded that neither, death, nor life nor angels, nor principalities or powers, nor things present or things to come, neither height nor depth nor any other creation shall be able to separate us from the love of God which is in Christ Jesus our Lord.

Be ready Saint!

Jesus has already won the battle!

SATAN'S A SUBTLE SO AND SO

We must be very careful,
Of what we say and what we hear.....
For Satan has a way,
Of softly whispering in our ear.

At first it's just a whisper,
Oh, so soft and low.....
In fact we may not hear a sound,
For he's a subtle so and so.

Ever so slowly we find ourselves,
Starting to feel low down....
And we may suddenly begin to gripe,
And criticize everyone around.

For Satan's favorite battleground,
Is the mind of the believer.....
But all of God's children know,
He's known as the great deceiver.

You know an evil thought,
Can quickly... become and evil deed.....
And if we let him have a foothold,
Soon he'll take the lead.

Satan loves to attack,
Through our vivid imagination.....
And he'll take sure advantage,
Of any freely given situation.

So bring every thought into captivity,
To the obedience of Christ.....
For allowing our minds to wander,
We may have to pay a very high price.

Cast out every imagination,
Contrary to God's will and to His word.....
And when Satan starts to whisper,
Just pretend you haven't heard.

SATAN'S A SUBTLE SO AND SO *Continued...*

He may keep on attacking,
Until his voice is like a roar.....
But if you keep on resisting,
Then his throat will get sore.

Read God's word...claim His promises,
And that old Devil will have to retreat.....
Shout Hallelujah...in the name of Jesus,
Then you'll know you've got him beat.

1985

HOPE

Dear One, have you ever felt like everything just seems so hopeless. You sometimes allow yourself to get down and discouraged and you can't understand what's wrong, and it's as if you have lost hope.

But hope is believing Jesus' and Father God's love for us will last forever. It is an unconditional love for us that will last for all eternity.

It's believing that just as our Father has promised, He is coming back to pick us up someday soon, when we least expect it.

Hope is really believing with all our hearts that the person we've been praying for all these years, is going to come to know Christ any day now.

It's believing until a person takes their last breath, that Jesus still saves and heals and that by His stripes we are healed spiritually and physically.

Hope gives the believer peace in the midst of the storms of life. And peace that the Lord will take us home to glory when our days on earth come to an end.

Don't lose hope my friend, it's all we have. And remember the One you have put your faith and trust in and it gives you hope.

HOPE

Lord, what is hope?
Is it not believing in a love that has no end....
Believing that one day soon, when we least expect it.....
From out of Your heaven You'll descend?

You'll descend...to pick up Your children,
And then You'll take us home to glory....
To live in peace forever,
Just as we were told in the old, old story.

Is it not believing you've forgiven me,
For all the folly of my youth?
And claiming all Your promises.....
As my only truth.

Is it not praying with all my heart,
For that lost soul.....
And believing that one day soon,
They'll give You full, complete control?

It must be believing in Your healing stripes,
As well as Your death on the cross.....
For my physical and spiritual healing,
Since You paid the cost.

Faith is the substance of things hoped for,
And the evidence of things not seen.
So that even in the midst of turmoil......
It's peaceful and serene.

2006

Dear Saint of God, Without hope there is no hope! Without hope life is hopeless and there is really no reason to live. Jesus is our hope, our joy and our peace.

EASTER LOVE

Dear Saint of God, Easter is such an awesome, thought provoking holiday. If people would just stop and think about what our God has done for us. Sending His precious Son (Christmas) to be born in a manger and to live a life of physical abuse and suffering and then to die the most horrible death (Easter)on a cruel cross. And to think our Father did this for us with no strings attached.

Christ died on the cross of Calvary not only for you and me but when you think that He also died for the ones who were laughing and mocking Him as He died, the very ones who were physically nailing Him to that cross. Such love we cannot comprehend. But when we want to judge the ones who did the act of nailing Him to the cross, we must stop and remember it was our sin, and the sins of the whole world that actually nailed our Savior to the tree.

Easter is so commercial today. People buy little bunnies and chicks that in a few weeks will be unwanted, they buy candy that no one needs to eat, they buy new clothes to wear to church, and yet the real meaning of Easter like Christmas is slipping away. Many people who never set foot in church all year, suddenly feel like going to church for Easter. I guess they believe they're giving something back to God for what He's done for them. How sad for many it's one hour a year.

Let's remember Easter all year through. Let's remember what our Savior willingly went through for us; and can we not willingly sacrifice some of our T.V. time or book reading or newspaper reading or sports or other time in order to read His Word, pray and go to church and fellowship with other believers? Remember, when we do sacrifice anything for the Lord, He always replaces it with more and better.

So, let's remember Easter 365 days a year and thank our Father everyday for the sacrifices He and His Son Jesus have made for us, and let us show our appreciation by in turn sacrificing our lives for the Lord, by dying to self and letting Jesus live through us, and in turn glorify Himself through us.

What a privilege to serve the King of Kings!

EASTER LOVE

Easter is not just hiding eggs,
And then looking everywhere.....
It's not just fuzzy bunnies,
With pink noses and white hair.

It's not the beautiful lilies,
And flowers of the spring.....
It's not the sunny day,
Nor the song that robins sing.

It's the precious Lamb of God,
Stretched out on a cruel tree.....
Who willingly suffered and died,
For sinners like you and me.

Before He came to earth,
He knew His father's plan.....
That He would be the Savior,
Of every woman, child and man.

He knew how he would suffer,
But was willing to pay the cost.....
Willing to give His life,
So that He might save the lost.

Never before and never again,
Will we ever find such love....
As the Father lavished upon us,
From He's throne in heaven above.

Would you send your son to suffer and die,
At the hands of cruel men.....
To open the door of heaven,
To such as the likes of them?

We're the very ones,
Who nailed Him to that tree.....
Yet He said, "Father, forgive them
As He died for you and me.

EASTER LOVE *Continued...*

Let's show how much we love Him,
By loving one another.....
By reaching out a helping hand,
To that sister or that brother.

Easter is not just one Sunday,
But it's 365 days a year....
So we need to share His love
With those both far and near.

2005

Share His love today friend, there are those who are dying for lack of love.

Topical Index

Comfort

He's Been There and He Cares	20
The Sweetness of His Presence	36
The Blessings of God	40
The Resting Place	50
I Love You	52
Through the Valley	54
To the End of Life's Journey	72
Trust Him	89
Going Home	96
No Higher Calling	100
This is Not Goodbye	119
Jesus I Love You	134
I'll Take and I'll Give	196
This Is Not Your Day	210
The Captain of Our Ship	216
Storms	218
You Shall Light My Candle	231
It's Over	240
Dear, Hurting Ones	242
He's Always There	268

Encouragement

Reflections of His Love	15
The Burning Bush	17
Save Me a Spot Right Next to You	29
Lead On, Dear Lord, Lead On	42
Don't Let Fear Get You Down	64
Rejoice My Downcast Soul	78
No Exchanges…No Returns	91
Diamond in the Rough	93
It's Raining	105
Peaks and Valleys	151
The Race	207
My Buried Treasure	246
Come Home	260
A Special Touch from You	275

Topical Index

Spiritual Growth

Do People See Jesus in Me?	22
The Way of Your Choosing	31
When Do We Call?	45
My Heart's Desire	59
Only God Can Change His Heart	69
Rush, Busy, Hurry	76
Humble Pie	98
Don't Live Your Life on Your Emotions	103
No Room	122
Resisting Satan	126
Our Secret	130
Can You Praise Him?	132
Letting Go	140
Love the Unlovely	142
What Is Our Motive?	147
My Boss	149
Take My Life and Use It	155
Feelings	160
Life Is Just So Busy, Lord	163
The Blood Is Here to Stay	171
Our Children	177
Tears	179
Pray	188
A Fit Vessel	199
Loss Is Sometimes Gain	204
Total Surrender	213
Have We Come So Far that We've Forgotten?	228
Religion in a Box	233
Sometimes I Don't Feel Saved	238
The Lesson of Love	248
I'm a Know-So	253
It Was Such a Small Thing	258
Is Your Heart Right?	271

Miscellaneous

The Love of God	12
At the Foot of the Cross	24
The Flower of Life	27
A Friend	34

Topical Index

Lord Fill Me Up	38
The Question	47
Happy Birthday, Jesus	57
The Glory Train	62
Jesus' Gentle Hands	66
The Hand of God	74
Momma of Mine	81
My Guardian Angel	83
Crystal Drops	86
The Butterfly	108
Daddy	110
Lawd, I Been a 'Tryin	112
My Friend, This is My Prayer for You	114
I Was Made for You, Lord	116
Let Them Remember	124
Let Us Be Thankful	137
Meme	145
The Little Thorny Briar	157
Praise Time	166
Take Me in Return	169
I Wonder Who's Watching	174
The Thief	182
All Is Not Right	185
Lord Show My Friend the Way	190
Making Memories	193
The Real Meaning of Christmas	201
Safe in the Arms of Jesus	221
Bundles of Joy	223
Is Something Missing from Your Life?	225
Christmas Hustle Bustle	236
The Master Painter	244
Yesterday, Today and Tomorrow	250
Slowdown and Remember	255
I Take the Blame	263
As We See Strangers Passing By	266
Time Is Slipping Away	273
Satan's a Subtle So and So	277
Hope	280
Easter Love	282

Printed in the United States
115425LV00001B/127-135/A